SOCIAL MIX AND THE CITY

Challenging the Mixed Communities Consensus in Housing and Urban Planning Policies

KATHY ARTHURSON

Flinders University

PUBLISHING

National Library of Australia Cataloguing-in-Publication entry

Arthurson, Kathy (Kathryn Diane)

Social mix and the city: challenging the mixed communities consensus in housing and urban planning policies/by Kathy Arthurson.

9780643096424 (pbk.)
9780643104440 (epdf)
9780643104457 (epub)

Includes bibliographical references and index.

Marginality, Social.
Globalization – Social aspects.
Urbanization – Social aspects.
Housing policy – Social aspects.

305.56

Published by

CSIRO PUBLISHING
36 Gardiner Road, Clayton VIC 3168
Private Bag 10, Clayton South VIC 3169
Australia

Telephone: [+613] 9545 8555
Local call: 1300 788 000 (Australia only)
Fax: +61 3 9662 7555
Email: csiropublishing@csiro.au
Web site: www.publishing.csiro.au

Front cover image by iStockphoto

Set in Adobe Minion Pro 11/13.5 and Adobe Helvetica Neue LT Std
Edited by Anna Cutler
Cover and text design by James Kelly
Typeset by Desktop Concepts Pty Ltd, Melbourne
Printed by Ingram Lightning Source

Feb26_RP_ILS

Contents

Acknowledgements

I want to dedicate this book to the following. First, to my dear Dad, who taught me to value perfection and honesty in everything I attempt. Second, to Graham, my partner, who helps me to lead a more balanced life than I might otherwise choose. Third, to the residents of the three case study neighbourhoods who gave up their time so generously in agreeing to be interviewed and allowing their views to form part of this book.

I also want to acknowledge the journals that published some of my earlier work on social mix in a series of articles, along with a book chapter. Some aspects of these have been reworked, revised, updated and expanded for this book:

Arthurson K (2008) The role of qualitative research in identifying residents' perspectives about social mix. In *Qualitative Housing Analysis: An International Perspective.* (Eds P Maginn, S Thompson and M Tonts) pp. 209–225. Emerald, Bingley, UK.

Arthurson K (2008) Australian public housing and the diverse histories of social mix. *Journal of Urban History* **34**(3), 484–501.

Arthurson K (2005) Social mix and the city, practice review. *Urban Policy and Research* **23**(4), 519–523.

Arthurson K (2002) Creating inclusive communities through balancing social mix: a critical relationship or tenuous link? *Urban Policy and Research* **20**(3), 245–261.

1

Introduction

Over the past 30 years, Australia and other developed nations have experienced lengthy periods of robust economic growth and increased prosperity. The current instability in the global economy, which began at the end of 2007, and issues of environmental sustainability, given the finite nature of many natural resources, suggests that the levels of economic growth experienced in the past is unlikely to be maintained into the future (Hamilton and Denniss 2005). This increased wealth and prosperity has not been shared equally by all members of society, as evidenced by problems of social polarisation, in which residents characterised by intergenerational unemployment, poverty, crime and antisocial behaviour are concentrated in particular neighbourhoods. The most visible of these neighbourhoods, but by no means all of those characterised by socioeconomic distress, are areas of high concentrations of social housing. The media has given extensive coverage to the recent riots in Rosemeadow, Macquarie Fields and Redfern social housing estates in Sydney, New South Wales. The media representations of a socially excluded underclass have often problematised the issues of disadvantaged neighbourhoods, narrowing the debates to discussions about the social housing tenure. Specifically, through redefining the problems of disadvantaged communities as due to the homogeneity or lack of 'social mix' of residents, with dramatic headlines, such as 'Housing policy "will create trust ghettos"' (Bildstien 2005). However, it is important to point out that despite this focus of debates about social mix on areas of concentrated social housing, concentrations of disadvantaged households also exist in private rental housing, which do not receive the same attention. The omission of private rental from the social mix literature is problematic, as in Australia and elsewhere most poor renters are in private rental and not in public housing, and some of our most deprived areas have virtually no public housing (Australian Bureau of Statistics 2008; Yates 2008).

What is social mix and how might we define it? In the modern-day context, social mix is generally used to refer to the lack of variance in housing tenure or socioeconomic status. These terms refer respectively to the balance between social housing renters, homeowners and private renters, and middle-income and low-income residents within a particular spatially defined area. In delineating its usage, though, social mix is an ambiguous concept and it is not always clear exactly what is meant when it is utilised by different stakeholders. This makes it difficult to neatly classify its attributes. Social mix is frequently used interchangeably as a term to refer to housing tenure and socioeconomic mix. What is clear is that, although social mix and housing tenure mix are often used as substitute terms, they are not the same thing. Changing the housing tenure mix within a neighbourhood may not, for instance, lead to expected changes in socioeconomic mix. A pertinent example is the situation in which social housing tenants purchase homes through urban renewal projects. What ensues is a similar socioeconomic mix of residents as before but with a mix of housing tenures in the form of homeowners and social housing renters. Social mix is also sometimes used to characterise a mix of age groups. This aspect, for instance, is utilised in referring to the mix of youth and aged residents in different high-rise social housing towers, blocks of flats or groups of units. At other times, the term is used to describe the variation in the ethnic mix of residents, although this adaptation appears less common in Australia than internationally.

The debates around social polarisation and spatial segregation between different socioeconomic groups, and the perceptions of the problematic nature of concentrations of disadvantaged residents in particular neighbourhoods have prompted renewed interest by governments in Australia and internationally in 'social mix policies'. These policies aim to reduce and reorder concentrations of the most disadvantaged members of neighbourhoods to create communities with a blend of residents across different housing tenures and with a variety of income levels. Intuitively for many government policymakers and urban planners, because concentration of disadvantage or homogeneity of residents with like characteristics within particular neighbourhoods is identified as a problem, the opposite situation, namely, heterogeneity, is seen as the pertinent solution. Attached to this ideal and drawn on to support policies to increase the social mix of neighbourhoods are expectations of improved life circumstances for disadvantaged residents.

While the title of this book stresses the city, most of the analysis will be centred on specific estates (neighbourhoods) of high concentrations of social housing where social mix policies are mainly focussed. The overall premise of this book is that we need to challenge the way debates about social mix and disadvantaged neighbourhoods are currently framed, rather than just ascribe to them. This chapter provides the background context and rationale for the book, introducing the major themes and outlining the structure for the chapters that follow.

The rationale for this book

Learning the lessons of history

Many of the contemporary debates about social mix tend to ignore the fact that ideas underlying planning for social mix have been around for a long time. There are some exceptions to this trend, such as the insightful work of Mark Peel (1993) on the planning and construction of the new town of Elizabeth by the South Australian Housing Trust (SAHT) in the late 1950s. His historical analysis demonstrates that attention to social mix informed the planning of new Australian towns and housing policy in the years after the Second World War. Building on Peel's historical analysis, a principal theme of this book is that the importance placed on social mix in planning and housing policy waxes and wanes over time. Policy goals, expectations about the problems they can address and meanings and values embedded in the concept of social mix also vary.

This book seeks to enhance our current understanding of the political and intellectual agendas for social mix by considering its comparative historical context and the purposes for which it is used. It is critical to unravel these different conceptualisations and uses because policies can be driven by different agendas, and if the underlying beliefs and assumptions are not placed in their historical context, we may be doomed to repeat past errors. One of the central questions tackled here is how to interpret the recent revived enthusiasm for social mix policies in late 20th and early 21st century Australia, including determining the forces behind the contemporary linking of social mix to debates about social exclusion on social housing estates. This question is impossible to comprehensively elucidate without commencing from an understanding of the historical origins of social mix policies and the different notions of the term over time. The policy intentions, logic and objectives of social mix policies will be scrutinised, paying close attention to questions of why and how social mix policies emerge at particular times. Without developing these sorts of understandings it is also difficult to envisage new conceptualisations of the policy process.

In brief, the origins of the concept of social mix can be identified in mid-19th century Britain. Some of the early advocates and influences on the development of the idea of social mix will be drawn on to explore the history of the concept, including Octavia Hill, George Cadbury's Bournville Village, and Ebenezer Howard's garden city movement. The development of social mix policies in Australia in the 1950s and 1960s will be traced through to the re-emergence in the present day where social mix is a popular notion in neighbourhood regeneration policy. From this perspective, the book tackles a major gap in knowledge within the debates about social mix through exploration of the way the social mix concept has been used historically. It explores explanations of the meanings and values that underlie the associations between social mix and housing and planning policy, and the way the intellectual and policy debates have diminished or changed over time.

Conceptualising the expectations and evidence for social mix

The second aim of the book is to provide critical engagement with the literature and reconceptualise the debate about social mix away from a one-dimensional binary about propinquity of 'well-off' and 'poor' residents as a means for providing simplistic solutions to poverty and inequality. A key question is what are the principal arguments and debates underlying support for social mix. Contemporary policies to create social mix within particular neighbourhoods, for instance, are pursued by policymakers and planners convinced of the benefits. There is an assumption that spatial propinquity of poor and better off residents provides benefits, specifically for disadvantaged groups. As George Galster, a US expert on social mix, points out, one of the expectations of policymakers is that advantaged and disadvantaged groups will interact within socially engineered mixed-income neighbourhoods (Galster 2007). Other goals relate to expectations of reducing the stigma and poor reputations attached to particular neighbourhoods by balancing social mix. Some of the questions delved into in this book are, how have these underlying goals and expectations arisen, and are there any unintended consequences of these sorts of policies? The book challenges the contemporary consensus in housing and urban planning policies that social mix is an optimum planning tool. In particular, underlying rationales drawn on to support social mix policies are challenged, such as notions about role modelling and middle class leadership to integrate problematic residents into more 'acceptable' social behaviours.

Mixing methodologies

Another contention of this book is that much of the contemporary literature explores questions about the sizes and levels of the social and economic effects of social mix policies (the so-called 'neighbourhood effects' literature). These types of studies attempt to create and apply rigorous, quantitative measures and evaluations of the impact of different levels of social mix on various aspects of disadvantaged residents' lives, including their health, education and employment prospects (see, for instance, special editions of *Housing Studies* **17**(1), 2002; **18**(6), 2003 and *Urban Studies* **38**(12), 2001; **22**(5), 2007).

As important as these studies are in adding to our knowledge, as others point out, a focus on quantitative findings alone could be misleading. The nub of the issue is that a holistic and balanced understanding also requires qualitative exploration of the experiences of neighbourhood residents, which may reflect quite different experiences to those intimated by statistical associations (Gwyther and Possamai-Inesedy 2009). There is a contention that, in the past and present, the views of the people most affected by the changes are little reflected (Darcy 2007; Arthurson 2008). Thus far, there are few explanations of how residents interpret changes to social mix or even if they think it matters or may 'affect their decisions and therefore life chances' (Atkinson and Kintrea 2004: 20). It is critical to have in-depth qualitative explorations of the knowledge and day-to-day effects of social mix from the viewpoint of residents of neighbourhood regeneration areas that have undergone changes to social mix (Rose 2004). Galster (2003), a quantitative specialist, adds fuel to this debate, also arguing that more qualitative in-depth analyses are needed to complement the existing statistical work on social mix.

This book aims to provide alternative insights into social mix, building on and complementing the existing approaches, many of which commence from questions about the levels and sizes of effects. It provides a qualitative perspective, engaging with the points of view of those most affected by social mix policies, the residents of regenerated social housing neighbourhoods, reporting on the findings of research conducted in three case study neighbourhoods in South Australia.

Contextualising arguments about social mix

Finally, much of the literature that evaluates the effects of social mix originates from the United States (US) and United Kingdom (UK). In the US, social mix policies are generally designed to relocate low-income African American and Hispanic households from 'distressed' neighbourhoods of concentrated poverty to private rental housing in areas with a wider socioeconomic mix. There, the programs utilise housing vouchers to 'scatter' public housing tenants across more prosperous neighbourhoods using private rental housing. This policy direction reflects the enforcement in law of the rights of African Americans to live in white suburbs. These specific types of programs, exemplified in the 'Gautreaux' and 'Moving to Opportunity' projects, have not developed in the Australian or UK context. The US debate about social mix is linked to notions of an 'urban underclass' and the idea that concentrations of social housing cause a culture of welfare dependency, social irresponsibility and problematic tenant behaviour. From this perspective, social mix policies are informed by the thesis that living among other similarly disadvantaged people detrimentally impacts on life chances and aspirations through the formation of a 'culture of poverty'. The culture of poverty thesis purports that individuals outside the labour market are generally culpable for their disadvantaged circumstances (Murray 1984, 1994).

In brief, in Australia and the UK, contemporary social mix policies aim to stimulate social mobility and inclusion. The policies, to date, adopted in Australia more closely resemble those of UK regeneration policy than the US. The UK approach focuses on regeneration *in situ* and aims for dilution of concentrations of social housing, often through private sales of social housing to existing tenants. In the UK and Australia, social mix is often implemented as part of a broader neighbourhood regeneration framework that acknowledges that where a person lives affects their access to important services and other opportunities, and may involve other initiatives, such as employment and community development projects.

Hence, although the US evidence base is often drawn on to support implementation of social mix policies in Australia, at the heart of social mix policies are different explanations and social and political contexts for how poverty arises and is best addressed. Thus far, there has been only limited exploration of how social mix policies work here in Australia, and to address this lacuna the book analyses the unique Australian experience of social mix.

Structure of the book

Part one

The first half of the book, from Chapter 2 to Chapter 5, sets out the historical context of social mix, exploring the concept from 19th century Britain to the present day. Taking this approach provides a way to ground the analysis, trace key debates about social mix, compare and contrast common themes and conceptualisations, and clarify changes over time to establish shifts in meaning and highlight their application in different situations.

Chapter 2: The origins of the concept of social mix

Chapter 2 traces the origins of the concept of social mix in town planning in Britain from the mid-19th century and touches on its implementation later in the US. The interpretation concentrates on the UK experience because this has been the most influential in forming Australian conceptualisations. The commentary includes an exploration of the early advocates and influences on the development of the idea of social mix, such as Octavia Hill and George Cadbury. Fundamental questions that are addressed include: what are the historical foundations of the idea of social mix, what problems was it initially constructed to address and who constructed these problems?

Chapter 3: Post-war debates

This chapter explores the growth in support for social mix policies and the ways in which they were conceptualised in the era after the Second World War of reconstruction and economic boom times. In particular, this chapter considers new town planning debates about social mix in Australia from the 1950s to 1970s drawing on the visions for the suburb of Elizabeth and the development of other mixed-tenure housing neighbourhoods at Salisbury North and Mitchell Park in South Australia. It also pays close attention to the criticisms and questioning of the value of the concept at this stage, which in part led to the declining interest in social mix policies in the decades immediately following the 1970s.

Chapter 4: 21st century debates: social mix, estate regeneration and social exclusion

In this chapter, the question of how to interpret the recent revived enthusiasm for social mix is explored. Key questions include: what are the forces behind the contemporary linking of social mix to social inclusion on social housing estates and what are the various meanings that underlie and are contained in the concept? The various rationales underlying support for social mix policies are examined including notions of role modelling and middle class leadership through propinquity to integrate problematic residents into more 'acceptable' social behaviours.

Chapter 5: Great expectations and the unexpected consequences of social mix policies

This chapter considers the ways in which the principal debates about social mix were constructed in the academic literature between 1990 and 2009, when the present review was completed. The second half of the chapter then turns to a discussion of some of the more practical and unexpected consequences of the implementation of social mix policies, which have received less attention in the debates.

Part two

The second half of the book, from Chapter 6 to Chapter 8, provides the background context and findings from the empirical study of the experiences of social mix policies of the residents themselves. While social mix is often accepted as a *fait accompli* in urban planning and housing policy circles, this section of the book challenges the consensus that changing social mix is an optimum planning tool. It achieves this by critically examining some of the underlying assumptions about social mix policies, specifically, claims of reductions in localised stigma and increases in social cohesion associated with lowering concentrations of social housing in particular neighbourhoods.

Chapter 6: Mixed-tenure neighbourhoods reconstituted

In this chapter, some of the more specific background context is provided for the case studies on social mix conducted in three neighbourhoods – Mitchell Park, Hillcrest and Northfield – all located in the metropolitan region of Adelaide, South Australia. These three neighbourhoods, which were previously characterised by high levels of socioeconomic disadvantage and high concentrations of social housing, have been revitalised over the past 20 or so years with extensive changes made to the social mix of the areas.

Chapter 7: Neighbourhood reputation, stigma and social mix

This chapter draws on findings from interviews with residents, gathered from the case studies of the three neighbourhoods. It explores residents' discourses about the impact of changes to social mix in neighbourhood regeneration on the reputation and stigma of the neighbourhoods. In particular, the similarities and differences between the perceptions of social housing tenants, homeowners and private renters are explored.

Chapter 8: Sense of community, social cohesion and social mix

As in the previous chapter, this chapter draws on in-depth interviews to present the perspectives of residents. However, in this situation the exploration is concerned with their judgements about the relationships between social mix and the sense of community and social cohesion within the three mixed-tenure neighbourhoods. Four major discourses emerged in the interviews and these encompassed residents' feelings of: sense of community and closeness of the neighbourhood; friendliness and friendships; perspectives on sharing the same or different values and tolerance of any differences; and trust and willingness to help neighbours.

Chapter 9: Conclusions

The final chapter draws together conclusions from the historical analysis and qualitative research and outlines implications for applying contemporary social mix policies.

References

Arthurson K (2008) Australian public housing and the diverse histories of social mix. *Journal of Urban History* **34**, 484–501.

Atkinson R and Kintrea K (2004) Opportunities and despair, it's all in there. *Sociology* **38**, 437–455.

Australian Bureau of Statistics (2008) 'Measuring Australia's progress: the headline indicators'. Australian Bureau of Statistics, Canberra, <http://www.abs.gov.au/AUSSTATS/abs@.nsf/allprimarymainfeatures/38E10976DF64EE07CA2574D30012FF70?opendocument>.

Bildstien C (2005) Housing policy 'will create trust ghettos'. *Advertiser* 24 March, p. 15.

Darcy M (2007) Place and disadvantage: the need for reflexive epistemology in spatial social science. *Urban Policy and Research* **25**, 347–361.

Galster G (2003) Investigating behavioural impacts of poor neighbourhoods: towards new data and analytic strategies. *Housing Studies* **18**, 893–914.

Galster G (2007) Neighbourhood social mix as a goal of housing policy: a theoretical analysis. *International Journal of Housing Policy* **7**, 19–43.

Gwyther G and Possamai-Inesedy A (2009) Methodologies à la carte: an examination of emerging qualitative methodologies in social research. *International Journal of Social Research Methodology* **12**, 99–115.

Hamilton C and Denniss R (2005) *Affluenza: When Too Much Is Never Enough.* Allen and Unwin, Sydney.

Murray C (1984) *Losing Ground, American Social Policy 1950–1980.* Basic Books Inc., New York.

Murray C (1994) *Underclass: The Crisis Deepens.* Institute of Economic Affairs, London.

Peel M (1993) A place made poor. *Arena Magazine* December 1993–January 1994, pp. 36–39.

Rose D (2004) 'The uneasy cohabitation of gentrification and social mix? A case study of residents of infill condominiums in Montreal.' Working paper. INRS-Urbanisation Culture et Société, Montreal.

Yates J (2008) Australia's housing affordability crisis. *Australian Economic Review* **41**(2), 200–214.

2

The origins of the concept of social mix

Introduction

Social mix, and specifically the use of the term in relation to housing tenure, has emerged as a key contemporary policy issue in Australia and internationally. However, one of the principal aspects missing from recent accounts is an exploration of the relevance of the notion of social mix in a historical sense. The contemporary academic debates and fervour for social mix in policy circles tend to ignore the fact that interest in social mix is by no means new. The concept has been around for a long time and the origins of the ideas underlying its adoption in Australian planning and housing policies can be identified in mid-19th century Britain. Three distinct periods are discernible in UK housing and urban planning policy when social mix emerged as a dominant discourse. The first period was in mid-19th century Britain when social mix was linked to utopian visions of reuniting the different social classes that were divided by the effects of industrial capitalism. Discourses about social mix were again reinvigorated in the economic boom time of the period after the Second World War when the debates were linked to egalitarian ideals and the achievement of social justice. In more recent times, the idea of social mix has become linked to addressing the problems of social exclusion arising in neighbourhoods of concentrated social housing (Cole and Goodchild 2000; Arthurson 2008).

Contemporary social mix policies affect social housing tenants living on estates that represent some of the most marginalised groups in Australian and other

Western societies. Thus, it is important to understand the different ways in which social mix policies have been conceptualised and adapted over time. Policies are driven by different agendas and interest groups, and if the underlying beliefs and assumptions are not placed in their historical context, we may be doomed to repeat past errors. The focus of this chapter is largely on exploring the origins of social mix policies in Britain because the ideas and concepts that emerged there in the mid to late Victorian era of the 19th century have been the most influential in the later adoption of social mix policies in Australian housing and urban planning policies. Before turning to this task, the question of why contemporary debates about social mix place little importance on historical analysis, including its origins, conceptualisations and varied uses is examined. The discussion then turns to an exploration of its historical origins, examining the early advocates and influences on the development of the concept in Britain, the different ideals that have helped to constitute the various meanings of 'social mix' and the ways in which it was constructed and adapted by different groups to deal with particular problems at certain junctures in time.

Why is historical analysis about social mix lacking?

Back in the mid-1970s, Sarkissian (1976) pointed out that the idea of social mix has existed for a long time. She traced the origins of social mix schemes to 19th century utopian visionaries and paternalistic factory owners. They eschewed the industrial city and yearned for an idealised and romanticised life that was presumed to exist in pre-industrial society; the notion of socially mixed villages where different classes coexisted harmoniously, the gentry living alongside the baker and artisans. Another strand of thought was utilitarian, as the new industrial cities were segregated by class and income and it was thought that mixed communities would function better and raise the standards of living of the poor through contact and emulation of the middle classes. Later, Australian work by Peel (1995) also situated ideas about social mix in a historical context, specifically exploring its links to the South Australian Government's housing and urban planning policies implemented in the 1950s. Peel's study of the development of the new town of Elizabeth by the SAHT is discussed in Chapter 3, which considers some of the dominant debates after the Second World War around social mix. Nevertheless, the majority of the preceding and contemporary 21st century debates about social mix do not treat it as a historical concept. Along with Peel, another exception to this tendency is the work of Cole and Goodchild (2000), whose analysis contrasts notions of social mix in the government policy discourses in Britain immediately following the Second World War with the more recently applied Blair New Labour Government policies that emerged from 1997 onwards. Goodchild and Cole (2001) illustrated that the concept of social mix is multilayered, drawing on the analogy of peeling the different layers of an onion to reveal diverse conceptualisations and meanings. In the case of social mix, the conceptualisations are dependent on the various levels of social reality from which it is viewed. Specifically, they found that the discourses about social mix varied at the broad level of national policy, at the level of management and regeneration of social housing estates and at the level of the social experience of residents. In combination, this body of work demonstrates the important point that the meanings attached to social mix are reconstituted and reimagined by different interest groups and under different social and historical circumstances.

In part, the contemporary lack of attention to the history of social mix may reflect the situation in which much of the current research on the topic is concerned with answering the policy-related question: does a balanced social mix achieve the anticipated results? If we start from the question is the policy working, the imperative is to measure and understand the social and economic effects of social mix in this particular instance or a fixed point in time. This type of approach conceals the importance of commencing from explaining its historical use and significance and the competing arguments that have shaped and formed the development of ideas about social mix historically. There is a substantial contemporary literature from the US, for instance, that is based around questions of whether change in neighbourhood social mix leads to improvements in residents' health, education or employment prospects (see, for example, Galster and Zobel 1998; Galster 2003). A series of these studies utilised random controlled experimental design to evaluate the 'Moving to Opportunity' and 'HOPE IV' mobility programs. These programs relocate poor African American and Hispanic families from inner city neighbourhoods of concentrated poverty and racial segregation to more prosperous middle-income neighbourhoods with a wider social mix. This form of research often attempts to measure and evaluate the levels and sizes of the effects on disadvantaged residents' lives in areas of concentrated poverty compared with neighbourhoods with a more variable tenure and income mix. The research design is characterised by the so-called objective, scientific method. One of the key characteristics is that participants are randomly allocated to different experimental groups to compare several interventions. Allocation of participants to the various groups is by chance, for instance, using a computerised lottery system. These studies may include comparing a control group of residents that remain living in public housing and in neighbourhoods with high concentrations of poverty, with a number of experimental groups that move to other more mixed-income neighbourhoods. To illustrate, in some cases an experimental group was provided with vouchers that could be used to move to housing in a more socioeconomically mixed neighbourhood with lower poverty rates. For this group, a non-profit organisation provided support in the form of counselling and assistance with finding suitable rental housing in neighbourhoods with low levels of poverty. Another group received standard vouchers that could be utilised in any neighbourhood but did not receive other specialised assistance. The control group remained living in the highly concentrated public housing neighbourhoods. The aim of these kinds of studies is to compare outcomes for each group of participants to ascertain the effects, on a continuum, of a range of social mix interventions.

Other statistical modelling studies of social mix draw on secondary data sources for their quantitative analysis, such as census and panel data. Like the evaluations of the US mobility programs, these sorts of studies also attempt to model and objectively measure the social and economic effects of social mix through manipulating the pertinent variables. An example of this type of study design is a study by Massey and Kanaiaupuni (1993), in the US context, which considered the question of whether public housing causes poverty concentrations. The researchers utilised a complex four-equation statistical model drawing on data from the Chicago standard metropolitan statistical area data set. The four equations sought to predict the:

(1) extent to which neighbourhood socioeconomic and racial composition was related to the likelihood of receiving public housing;
(2) effect public housing location had on creating poverty in particular neighbourhoods;
(3) effect of concentrated poverty and public housing on net migration out of the neighbourhoods; and
(4) impacts of net migration and public housing project location on the concentration of poverty.

The researchers concluded that public housing projects initially targeted poor African American neighbourhoods, and that in later years the presence of the projects increased the concentration of poverty. Importantly, their work enumerates the extent of racial segregation of poor African American families in particular neighbourhoods in the US, and in doing so also draws attention to important contextual differences between Australian and US social mix policies. However, this sort of analysis only tells part of the story as it is unable to explicate the political, social, historical and personal issues attached to the experiences of racial segregation and lack of social mix and how these situations arise.

Some of the contemporary studies concerned with social mix concentrate more on exploring aspects of residents' everyday experiences, drawing on fieldwork approaches and utilising particular neighbourhoods as case studies. This design sometimes involves comparative studies across different neighbourhoods. The various analyses explore residents' social networks and social interactions and how these vary across different housing tenures for homeowners, private renters and social housing tenants (e.g. Rosenbaum *et al.* 1998; Atkinson and Kintrea 2004;

Ruming *et al.* 2004). There is no questioning that, collectively, the different sorts of studies have led to valuable information with which to inform contemporary debate about social mix. However, as highlighted, there is currently a lack of acknowledgement of previous historical debates or explorations of the adoption of social mix by particular groups for different uses. The nub of the issue is that social mix is often treated as if it is a contemporary discovery rather than having a long and varied history.

In summarising the discussion thus far, part of the explanation for this anomaly is that the aim of much social mix research commences from policy-related questions, with the expectation of informing policymakers in their efforts to address social problems. While this is a worthy quest, some commentators drawing on their own experiences of conducting housing research argue that it then becomes difficult to identify alternative conceptualisations of the policy process. The resultant research is often 'methodologically conservative' and does little to highlight how policies reflect the outcomes of competing claims of different pressure groups with certain issues becoming defined as problems due to the way interest groups compete and debate with each other. Some issues gain particular dominant definitions of problems while others are rejected (Jacobs and Manzi 2000: 87). It is important to look at these different concepts to understand how policies arise, what uses they are put to and the underlying values, beliefs and agendas that drive them. Another explanation for why the historical dimension of social mix has received little attention in contemporary debates is that the focus of much research on social mix is on the here and now, so limited attention has been paid to questions of why and how policies have emerged or have been adapted historically. One way forward is to examine the relevance of the concept of social mix lineage through history by investigating the dominant debates about social mix and its use in policy and practice. Taking this approach provides a basis from which to scrutinise changes in the policy and intellectual discourses, assumptions, meanings and interpretations of social mix over time.

This chapter next turns to exploring the historical basis of social mix policies in mid-19th century Britain and different notions of the term that have been utilised. These notions provide important historical context, which formed the basis for later adoption of ideas about social mix in Australian housing and urban planning. The analysis seeks to contribute to both knowledge and understanding of the notion of social mix. It will pay close attention to how the idea of social mix was originally constructed, thereby laying the foundations for the explorations that follow in the rest of the book into how it has been adapted over time as a tool for dealing with the concentrations of impoverished residents on social housing estates. The aim is to trace where similar or different ideas about social mix have evolved or dissipated over time, and which groups were advocating them and for what particular intents and purposes.

Nineteenth century Britain: foundations of the concept of social mix

In the mid-19th century, British intellectuals and social activists were concerned with addressing the declining urban quality of towns and cities and the spatial segregation that had developed between the classes as a result of rapid industrialisation. The invention of factory machinery rendered workers in cottage industries redundant and the expansion of the global economic system lowered the market price of agricultural goods, undercutting the ability of small-scale farmers to survive economically. In turn, as workers competed for the limited available work, capitalist owners were able to keep wages low (Clark 2003). As destitute families flocked to the industrial towns in search of work, the towns became overcrowded and noisy, and housing and sanitary conditions were inadequate to cope with the population influx. As the condition of the towns deteriorated further, the upper and middle classes began to vacate these areas to reside in the countryside, resulting in the working classes becoming concentrated in inner city slums. Engels (1892), in his classic work on the condition of the working class, vividly depicts the poverty and health problems of the poor living in London and other great towns. The towns are described as filthy slums, characterised by rotting food, people living in poverty and dying from starvation and disease, with overcrowding, inadequate housing, air pollution due to poor ventilation in houses and coal smoke, and a lack of sanitation and adequate water supplies. Thus, the industrial towns and cities and their undesirable social and sanitary conditions were commonly associated with increasing concentrations of working class people (Glass 1972). While the concerns voiced at this time were about class segregation and the divisions between rich and poor, the proposed solutions became linked to the provision of housing and the planning of towns and cities.

This section examines the rationales underlying the development of four models for providing housing and planning for towns and cities with social mix, to illustrate some of the dominant ideas of the time adopted by social activists. Social activists linked housing and social mix in practice as a solution to address the spatial class segregation and worsening social, health and economic conditions of the late 19th century. The prototypes are model industrial villages, the provision of rental housing for the poor, the garden city movement and university settlements.

Model industrial villages

A number of social reformers in 19th century Britain believed that one of the best ways to deal with the problems of polluted industrial towns and cities was to relocate factory production from the inner city to greenfield sites outside the cities in order to build new communities or model towns. The idea was that these model industrial villages would provide a planned residential environment to encourage a balanced social mix across different classes while maintaining traditional hierarchies and a sense of identity with the company and village life. The principles of model villages were espoused by reformers, such as Robert Owen, who in the early 19th century proposed building villages encompassing manufacturing and agriculture to accommodate a limited number of persons (between 1000 and 1500) to avoid the problems of overcrowding in the cities. All of the needs of the community were to be contained within the immediate geographical area including access to schooling and employment. Others proposed similar communities, such as James Silk Buckingham's 10 000 person settlement to be named Victoria, with an experimental mixed-class population including the provision of free schooling, mixed land use and a green belt encompassing the settlement. A number of small utopian communities were in progress between 1851 and 1871 including Saltaire, which was built by Titus Salt to replace his wool mills in Bradford with a single large factory and new town for the workforce.

George Cadbury, the industrial chocolate maker, incorporated many of the ideas of model villages when he founded his settlement of Bournville Village in 1895. His concept was broader than the others, in that it was not only a company town but aimed to present a model to society of how to provide decent standards of living for the working classes and still run a profitable company (Pacione 2005: 227). Bournville Village was a seminal project as it put the idea of residential social mix into practice (Sarkissian 1976). Cadbury developed Bournville Village with a view to improving the morality and health of his workers through providing clean living environments and a balanced residential mix in terms of occupation and class. As restated by the Bournville Village Trust, Cadbury aimed to:

> *Provide high quality housing developments, distinctive in architecture, landscape and environment, in socially mixed communities, using best management practices to promote ways to improve the quality of life for those living in such communities. (Bournville Village Trust 2004)*

Cadbury's aim to create socially mixed communities was enacted in the setting up of Bournville Village through vetting potential residents specifically to create a blend of income and class. At Bournville, the housing was designed so that the middle classes resided adjacent to the working classes. Implicit within the development of Bournville were two principal ideas about the benefits that socially mixed communities would provide for the working classes. First, there was an assumption that the working classes needed propinquity with the middle classes to provide role models of appropriate behaviour in order for them to become good citizens. From this perspective, the presence of middle-income residents was expected to instil a work ethic in the working classes and to educate them with middle class standards of behaviour together with improved standards of cleanliness and health-related behaviours to maintain a healthy and productive workforce (Sarkissian 1975: 30). Inextricably linked to these ideas, the vision for Bournville depicted a romanticised and idealised notion about recreating a pre-industrial village in an urban environment, with a view to producing mixed communities of classes and professions where everyone recognised their place on the social stratum (Sarkissian 1976).

The second rationale underlying the Bournville model originated from a fear of the poor and the related association of poverty with amoral and dangerous behaviour. As the classes became more spatially segregated, the middle and upper classes developed a distorted image of the working classes, who were often portrayed as threatening. The concentrations of working class residents within the towns and industrial cities were perceived as threats to social harmony, which was confirmed by sporadic riots (Glass 1972). From this viewpoint, dispersing the working classes to model villages, such as Bournville, under the direction of their employers was seen as a way to dispel the dangers of concentrating the working classes and what was perceived as their menacing presence. It was assumed that the different classes would coexist harmoniously. Although the model town of Victoria envisaged by James Silk Buckingham was never built, the ideas underpinning it, along with Cadbury's Bournville development, both influenced Ebenezer Howard in his creation of the garden city design.

Ebenezer Howard and the garden city movement

Ebenezer Howard's publication *Garden Cities of Tomorrow* (1902) (originally published 1898 in booklet form as *Tomorrow: A Peaceful Path to Real Reform*) was highly influential in the British and American planning fraternities (Geertse 2008). This publication detailed Howard's alternative model solution to the appalling living conditions experienced by the poor in London and other large towns. He proposed bringing together the best aspects of the countryside and the city through uniting the fresh air and nature of the countryside with the employment and social opportunities available in the city. Howard's vision was utopian and proposed community building effused with social justice and values of collective socialism to break free from the dictates of capitalist oppression. Aspects of his model included cooperatives for production, employment and exchange, collective land tenure and planned cities (Clark 2003: 90). Howard hoped the garden city would form part of a social reform movement as he believed in pensions for the old and infirm, social reform and social justice, and creating gardens instead of slums (Clark 2003).

Nonetheless, like many visionaries, some of the finer detail of how the social transformation would take place in this new urban environment was left to others to administer and put into practice. In implementing the first model garden city at Letchworth, the heterogeneous mix of Cadbury's Bournville, where workers and middle class residents lived adjacent to each other, was not replicated. Letchworth included a cross-section of society but represented a limited 'residential mix', much like that envisaged by Buckingham's settlement of Victoria, where there was segregation by income and class at finer scales of neighbourhood and block, while social mix was thus implemented at the broader town-wide scale. Although the design of the model villages influenced Howard's concept, the association with the model industrial communities in practice was a noticeable deviation from his original idea of self-contained communities, collective ownership of the means of production and workers cooperatives fostering mutual support. 'Howard's ideological outlook was submerged' by others involved in its implementation and merged with industrial settlements, approximating Bournville and Port Sunlight to make it more tangible (Geertse 2008: 3).

'Supportive' rental housing for the poor – Octavia Hill

In the late 19th century, the English social activist Octavia Hill supported ideas comparable to those espoused by the reformers advocating model industrial villages, such as the working classes benefiting from exposure to middle class values. However, her ideas were also shaped by the public health reform of that era. She was highly influenced by the perspectives of her grandfather, Dr Southwood Smith, an influential figure in the public health movement in the 1840s. During the 1830s and 1840s, life expectancy at birth in the new industrial cities reflected the human costs of economic development and urban overcrowding, and dropped to levels not experienced since the devastating years of the Black Death. Given her exposure to these viewpoints, Hill recognised the links between poor quality housing and poor quality health. With the financial backing of a benefactor, John Ruskin, Hill carried out improvements to housing, which she managed and rented out to disadvantaged tenants. The slum property she initially took on to manage was previously known as 'Little Hell'. Importantly, Hill's work showed that rehabilitating and improving housing for the poor were viable options to merely demolishing it (Ravetz 2001: 3, 29).

From Hill's viewpoint, the morals and living standards of the poor could improve through their exposure to the educated classes. However, Hill's ideas about the provision of housing and social mix differed from Bournville and the garden cities in that it was not deemed necessary for the different classes to live in close proximity. Alternatively, Hill aimed to bridge the gap between the classes by providing middle class role models and leadership, specifically with 'well-bred women' acting as volunteers and rent collectors to visit her working class tenants. She was reluctant to have the middle-income rent collectors live among the poor, perceiving that immersing them in poverty would cloud their judgement and result in the provision of charity rather than proper assistance. Initially, she collected the rent from her tenants in person. This was soon not feasible, as the number of houses grew from nine accommodating several dozen tenants, to hundreds of properties supporting 5000 tenants (Spain 2006). Hill then utilised a system of 'friendly rent collecting' where the rent, which was paid weekly, was collected by upper class women, forming the early beginnings of the modern-day social work movement (Adam 2002). The role of these visitors was to provide advice and assistance, such as 'supplying them with flowers, teaching them to grow plants, arranging happy amusements for them, and in every way helping them to help themselves' (Hill 1875: 35). Hill wanted to free her tenants from what she viewed as:

> *The corrupting effect of continual forced communication with degraded fellow lodgers; from the heavy accumulated dirt ... my strongest endeavours were to be used to rouse habits of industry and effort, without which they must finally sink ... The plan was one which depended on just governing more than helping. (Moberly Bell 1943)*

The Oxford settlers in London

Similar ideas to the other reformers about the benefits of social mix for providing middle class role models for educating the poor were encapsulated in the setting up of university settlements. Henrietta and Samuel Barnett set up Toynbee Hall in east London in 1884. Toynbee Hall united university teaching with adult education with the aim of closing the divide between the social classes, which was thought to be achievable through the educated classes spending time with and living among the poor. Henrietta Barnett was an acquaintance of Octavia Hill and had worked as a rent collector for Hill before setting up a women's university settlement where middle class women lived among the poor (Slack 1982). The university settlements were concerned with locating the educated classes among the working classes within the cities. The aim was to provide working class residents with the benefits of resident gentry, comparable to the clergymen or squire living in rural parishes, to inform the poor of middle class standards (Glass 1972: 66). Analogous to the development of Bournville Village, this depiction involved an idealised notion of the pre-industrial village with expectations that the different classes would coexist in social harmony. Once again, the insinuation was that the working classes did not know how to behave properly and needed to have exposure to the values and behaviours of the middle and upper classes to become good citizens. The ideas behind the establishment of the university settlements also reflected fears about the association of the poor with dirt, disorder and disease that emerged from the public health movement of that time and aimed to bridge the perceived class divides as reflected in the following decree:

> *It will be something if they create among a few, a distaste for dirt and disorder, if they make some discontented with their degrading conditions, if they level public*

> *opinion with the belief that the law which provides cleanliness, light and order should be applied equally in all quarters of the town.* (Barnett 1894: 104)

Similar ideas to these about the importance of propinquity of the classes were evoked by Henrietta Barnett in the related development of the garden city (suburb) of Hampstead. Here, it was envisaged that community would be built through the different classes living together and enabling social mix 'without artificial efforts to build bridges between one class and another' (Slack 1982). To enact this vision, Barnett approached Raymond Unwin and asked him to be the master planner for the suburb. At the time, Unwin was working on Letchworth, which was the practical expression of Ebenezer Howard's garden city. He was also the architect of another model village based on Howard's ideas that was commissioned by Joseph Rowntree and built at New Earswick on the outskirts of York. Nonetheless, Hampstead Gardens did not end up with the social mix that was envisioned by Barnett. Unwin argued for the necessity of avoiding concentrating residents of different classes in the same parts of the estate (Burnett 1986). The design of Hampstead also departed from the garden cities concept, as it was a suburb of London rather than a self-contained town. Although there was concern that people should mix across classes, the design of the suburb created different groupings, which arguably worked against this occurring. Houses for the skilled working classes were built in the north, and larger houses for the middle classes in the south, creating spatial class segregation within the suburb and minimal provision to accommodate unskilled workers. As demand for housing in Hampstead grew, especially given its proximity to the new tube station at Golders Green, the suburb developed into a middle class enclave. As the suburb was located in a desirable area of London, the type and cost of housing made it generally inaccessible for the working classes.

Conclusion

The concept of social mix has been around for a long time, at least from the mid-19th century in Britain. Social mix policies at that time were a localised response to the problems of social segregation between the classes that arose due to broader social and industrial change. The undesirable slum-like conditions in the towns and cities were associated with high concentrations of the working classes in those locations. At the heart of social mix policies at that time were a number of competing debates about the problems of spatial segregation of the classes, and how poverty arises and is best addressed.

A prominent discourse about social mix expressed fears that concentration of the working classes was a threat that would lead to class conflict and social disharmony. Social mix was conceived as a solution because it diluted the concentrations of the working classes, ruptured their social solidarity and deflected their perceived potentially threatening behaviours. A related debate focussed on the dirt, pestilence and contagion associated with the working class as the upper and middle classes became increasingly aware that they managed to avoid some of the epidemics that affected the poor (Szreter 2003). In an interconnected argument, the imperative to maintain the health and vitality of the working class as a labour force for industrial capitalism was stressed.

Another discourse about social mix advocated a mix of classes within the same locality, or utilising volunteer visitors as middle class role models to educate the working classes on appropriate models of behaviour than where the working classes were concentrated in one place. Clearly, 19th century social activists largely employed the concept of social mix in paternalistic ways in their efforts to create a more harmonious and orderly society, although Octavia Hill advocated self-development rather than charity. Often, these earlier charitable depictions of poverty thought it was up to the poor to 'pull themselves up by their own efforts' and did not 'recognise that the causes of poverty were systemic and societal rather than individual' (Ravetz 2001: 18). In all of these discourses, the use of social mix proffered a convenient device that targeted individual behaviour as the cause of problems of social and urban decline while leaving the existing hierarchical and inequitable social system intact.

In these accounts, history was predominantly written by the educated classes and the voices of the poor were largely missing. Instead, the reformers imposed their own viewpoints, making the assumption that they were familiar with what the poor desired or needed to improve their lives. As the royal commission in 1884 stated 'the inhabitants of the slums were not given a chance to tell their own story ... they were never consulted about the kind of help that would be most useful to them' (Ravetz 2001: 25, 26). Further, one of the Barnett's working class protégés expressed the view that the middle classes provided 'a bad example with their pleasure-loving sons and idle, vain daughters, always thinking of dressing, and avoiding natural duties as if they were sins' (Barnett 1894: 266). There also seemed little cohesion in these new socially mixed communities. In the garden city of Letchworth, for instance, the 'commercial types' (middle class) and 'simple lifers' (working class) avoided contact, and the workers had no ties to the community, stating that they missed their friends and meeting at the pub in their old east London dockside neighbourhood and felt uncomfortable in a community with a middle class that 'looked down on them' (Buder 1990: 91, 92). Conversely, the middle classes complained about working class vandalism and rowdiness.

Nevertheless, this model of planning neighbourhoods by trying to integrate the different classes through social mix was replicated across Britain and imported by US planners. At this stage, it was depicted as a way of trying to produce, through physical means, some productive encounters between the classes to provide role modelling for disadvantaged residents and to facilitate an overall sense of community. Interest in social mix slumbered between the two world wars until the idea was reinvigorated in the 1950s after the Second World War (Sarkissian 1976), which is the epoch for the discussion in the next chapter.

References

Adam T (2002) Transatlantic trading: the transfer of philanthropic models between European and North American cities during the nineteenth and early twentieth centuries. *Journal of Urban History* **28**, 328–351.

Arthurson K (2008) Australian public housing and the diverse histories of social mix. *Journal of Urban History* **34**, 484–501.

Atkinson R and Kintrea K (2004) Opportunities and despair, it's all in there. *Sociology* **38**, 437–455.

Barnett SA (1894) *Practicable Socialism: Essays on Social Reform*. Longmans, London.

Bournville Village Trust (2004) 'The development of Bournville, the factory and village in a garden'. <http//www.bwhs.org.uk/who-we-are/the-factory-in-a-garden-story/>.

Buder S (1990) *Visionaries and Planners: The Garden City Movement and the Modern Community*. Oxford University Press, New York.

Burnett J (1986) *A Social History of Housing 1815–1985*. 2nd edn. Methuen, London.

Clark B (2003) Ebenezer Howard and the marriage of town and country. *Organization & Environment* **16**, 87–97.

Cole I and Goodchild B (2000) Social mix and the 'balanced community' in British housing policy – a tale of two epochs. *GeoJournal* **51**, 351–360, doi: 10.1023/a:1012049526513.

Engels F (1892) *The Condition of the Working Class in England in 1844*. Cossimo Classics, New York.

Galster G (2003) Investigating behavioural impacts of poor neighbourhoods: towards new data and analytic strategies. *Housing Studies* **18**, 893–914.

Galster G and Zobel A (1998) Will dispersed housing programmes reduce social problems in the US? *Housing Studies* **13**, 605–622.

Geertse M (2008) 'Garden cities to the world! The international propagation of the garden cities idea'. In *Proceedings of the Seventh European Social Science History Conference*, 26 February–1 March. Lisbon, Portugal.

Glass R (1972) Anti-urbanism. In *The City: The Problems of Planning*. (Ed. M Stewart) pp. 63–71. Penguin Interdisciplinary Readings, London.

Goodchild BJ and Cole ID (2001) Social balance and mixed neighbourhoods in Britain since 1979: a review of discourse and practice in social housing. *Environment and Planning D: Society and Space* **19**(1) 103–121.

Hill O (1875) *Homes of the London Poor.* State Charities Aid Association, New York. Cambridge University Press: UK.

Howard E (1898) *Tomorrow: A Peaceful Path to Real Reform.* Swan Sonnenschein: London.

Howard E (1902) *Garden Cities of Tomorrow.* Swan Sonnenschein: London.

Jacobs K and Manzi T (2000) Performance indicators and social constructivism: conflict and control in housing management. *Critical Social Policy* **20**, 85–103.

Massey D and Kanaiaupuni S (1993) Public housing and the concentration of poverty. *Social Sciences Quarterly* **74**, 109–122.

Moberly Bell E (1943) *Octavia Hill, A Biography.* Constable, Leicester.

Pacione M (2005) *Urban Geography: A Global Perspective.* Routledge, London.

Peel M (1995) *Good Times, Hard Times. The Past and the Future in Elizabeth.* Melbourne University Press, Melbourne.

Ravetz A (2001) *Council Housing and Culture: The History of a Social Experiment.* Routledge, London.

Rosenbaum J, Stroh L and Flynn C (1998) Lark Parc Place: a study of mixed-income housing. *Housing Policy Debate* **9**, 703–740.

Ruming KJ, Mee KJ and McGuirk PM (2004) Questioning the rhetoric of social mix: courteous community or hidden hostility? *Australian Geographical Studies* **42**, 234–248, doi: 10.1111/j.1467-8470.2004.00275.x.

Sarkissian W (1975) A peaceful path to real reform? A critical review of the idea of social mix. Master of Town Planning thesis. University of Adelaide, South Australia.

Sarkissian W (1976) The idea of social mix in town planning: an historical overview. *Urban Studies* **13**, 231–246.

Slack KM (1982) *Henrietta's Dream: A Chronicle of Hampstead Garden Suburb 1905–1982.* Self published, London.

Spain D (2006) Octavia Hill's philosophy of housing reform: from British roots to American soil. *Journal of Planning History* **5**, 106–125.

Szreter S (2003) The population health approach in historical perspective. *American Journal of Public Health* **93**, 421–431.

3

Post-war debates

Introduction

In the early 20th century, interest in social mix seemed to wane (Sarkissian 1975: 28). The immediate reasons for this decline are unclear, but may be partly attributed to energy and resources being directed to the war efforts. This stage in history was also marked by the worldwide economic Great Depression. Nonetheless, social mix still had some supporters during and between the war years, such as Lewis Mumford, one of the leading 20th century American authorities on cities and modern architecture. Mumford argued strongly against segregation and propagated the idea of planned social mix based on his observations of the damage rendered by homogeneous slums that concentrated the poor and most disadvantaged members of society. From his perspective, it was not only important for the disadvantaged to have exposure to a variety of social environments, activities and different groups but it also resulted in more equitable outcomes. The nub of the issue was that, where diverse socioeconomic groups were located together, it seemed easier to secure finances for neighbourhood infrastructure and other needed facilities. Mumford's vision of social mix was epitomised by the socioeconomically mixed community of Sunnyside Gardens where he was a resident (Mumford 1938). Sunnyside was constructed in the 1920s in north-western Queens, New York City, and represented the first American adaptation of Ebenezer Howard's garden city design. A mix of housing types was constructed, encompassing row houses and apartments, which assisted in attracting a diverse socioeconomic mix of residents to the neighbourhood.

Mumford was an influential proponent for British planners, who were interested in adopting social mix policies after the Second World War.

In the British policy context, interest in social mix was reinvigorated in the years immediately after the Second World War, as debates arose about how to build a new society which reunited the sense of togetherness that was experienced during the war years. At this stage, social mix was perceived as a tool to support romanticised ideals about bonding of the different classes, as was facilitated through working together to advance a common cause during the wars. The re-emergence of discourse about social mix at this time was inextricably linked in a practical sense with post-war rebuilding programs, such as the New Towns built from 1945 to 1951 in Britain. Also of major significance were the far-reaching government reforms instigated during construction of the welfare state, which involved debates about universal service provision by the state (Cole and Goodchild 2000). Aneurin Bevan, the British Labour Minister of Health and Local Government in 1945, argued that providing universal access to public housing would achieve social balance within neighbourhoods, in contrast with the homogeneity that would result from targeting only the most disadvantaged groups. The discourses at this time reflected arguments about the importance of redistribution of wealth and other services from the better off to the less advantaged members of society. However, undertones of some of the earlier discourses that had arisen in Victorian England were also discernible. Specifically, arguments about social mix as a tool to support propinquity between rich and poor or different classes and as a means for providing middle class role models to educate the poor about the proper way to live in society. While 'social balance' was developing a privileged place in the discourses of British planning texts about neighbourhoods, the 'degree of mix' and practical methods for achieving it were not clearly articulated (Thornbury 1978). British ideas and perspectives about social mix permeated Australian planning circles, albeit imported to Australian shores at a later stage, not becoming apparent until the 1950s.

This chapter investigates the emergence of earlier British discourses about social mix in Australian planning and housing policies. In particular, the historical analysis draws on South Australian public housing policy, as this is the location of case studies used for the exploration of social mix policies discussed in the second half of the book. To unravel the Australian experience of social mix, it is first necessary to detail the development of Australian public housing, including a short history of the Commonwealth–State Housing Agreement, as this provides important context for why support for social mix arose in Australia in the 1950s. Then, the discussion turns to South Australia where the social democratic foundations of the development of the SAHT illustrate the early redistributive ideals surrounding social mix and the benefits thought to accrue to residents from its implementation. This investigation draws on earlier developed estates in South Australia. These encompass Salisbury

North, the first estate constructed in South Australia, which provided the blueprint for other developments that followed, including the new town of Elizabeth and the three estates reported here in case studies.

Housing policy and social mix (1950–60s)

The foundations of the Australian public housing system

When the Commonwealth Housing Commission was set up in 1943, one of its initial tasks was to conduct an inquiry into the condition of Australian housing. The inquiry found that demand for housing outstripped supply in all Australian states and that much of the existing housing was of poor quality. The shortage of housing resulted from the severe decline in construction during the 1930s depression and Second World War period. The Commission argued that to address these problems, at least 700 000 houses needed be built over the following decade (Sandercock 1977: 103–105). Based on the recommendations of the inquiry, the Commonwealth–State Housing Agreement (CSHA) was enacted in 1945 and then renegotiated every few years between the federal and state governments until the end of 2008, when it was superseded by the National Affordable Housing Agreement (NAHA). The new agreement has involved considerable change to the way the financial and policy framework for Australian social housing is structured, by offering tax and other funding incentives to encourage institutional investment in affordable housing. These new arrangements aim to avoid what are perceived as the current problems with social housing, including concentrations of housing in particular neighbourhoods, issues of stigma, lack of access to services and employment, and highly disadvantaged residents experiencing social exclusion. This change in policy direction is explored more fully in Chapter 4, which discusses the present-day debates about public housing and social mix.

Nonetheless, initiation of the CSHA in 1945 represented a significant commitment by the Australian Federal Government and the state governments to build a national framework for planning, coordination, delivery and funding of public housing. Within the parameters of the agreement, the states were made responsible for the provision of housing, mainly to accommodate low-income working groups. Reflecting its broader fiscal powers and duty to achieve national equity, the Commonwealth financed construction of public housing, initially by providing the states with low-interest loans. To address the demand at this time for decent, affordable and good-quality housing, a major public sector building program was implemented. Thus, in Australia, like Britain, the period immediately after the Second World War was also a time of nation building, with government construction of infrastructure and state welfare provision of social housing, health and other key services. The housing, to meet economies of scale, was mainly constructed as public housing estates on sizeable land holdings often located on the fringe areas of cities where land was relatively cheap. Notwithstanding this initial support for developing public housing, successive Australian governments have provided greater support for home ownership, which is also preferred by the electorate, rather than low-income public rental tenure. At the peak of public housing in 1966, 8% of all Australian dwellings were public rental (Hayward 1996); however, by international standards this level is modest, especially when compared with many European countries. Nevertheless, in the period of strong economic growth after the Second World War, public housing provided decent and affordable housing for a small but significant segment of the Australian population (Stretton 1975).

At the time of construction, in the 1950s and 1960s, public housing estates were built to house large families, mainly with sizeable backyards on one-quarter acre blocks of land. The housing was often mass-produced and homogeneous in design, characterised by concentrations of row after row of similar housing, making it readily identifiable from surrounding suburbs that grew up around it. In contrast, in Victoria and New South Wales much of the public housing was constructed as high-rise towers as part of 'slum reclamation' programs in inner city areas, following the UK model of social housing. This housing was clearly identifiable and was initially designed to house low-income families. At this time, social mix was not a consideration, as the housing was mono-tenure and was provided to accommodate low-income, working families. The target groups for contemporary public housing, which include those with substance abuse problems, homelessness, mental health issues and ex-prisoners, were at this stage ineligible to apply.

From 1945 to 1956, under successive renegotiations of the CSHA, Commonwealth governments placed restrictions on sales of public housing stock, allowing the tenure to grow quite rapidly in most Australian states. Conversely, the 1956 agreement allowed the sale of public dwellings and subsequently saw additional assistance provided to home ownership programs. Over the following decades, much of the best public housing stock was sold for home ownership (Paris 1985). However, despite the general principles underpinning the CSHA, there are some noteworthy differences in the way the state housing authorities evolved and developed public housing. To understand some of these variations in the development of public housing in the Australian states, discussion next turns briefly to a comparison of some of the differences between New South Wales, Queensland and South Australia. This comparison highlights the specific policy context for considering the three case studies, which are located in South Australia.

Different roles and uses of public housing in Australian states

New South Wales

The New South Wales Housing Commission, as well as providing rental housing, also acted as a development authority, with the first residences constructed in 1942 to house employees of munitions factories in the rural regions of Bathurst, Cowra,

Lithgow and Orange (New South Wales Department of Housing 2001). As in other Australian states, to meet demand for housing in the post-war period the housing authority purchased large land holdings and constructed broadacre estates with mass-produced housing built to economies of scale. This action resulted in approximately one-third of the public housing stock in New South Wales eventually being located on large estates (Darcy and Randolph 1999). Many of the estates were constructed in the outer metropolitan regions where land was cheaper and there were no planned industrial sites to provide employment or attract other services as part of the developments (Jones 1972). The New South Wales Housing Commission also played a major role as a slum clearance and rehousing authority, and much of the inner city public housing was built or acquired to regenerate slums. The first slum clearance began in the inner city suburb of Redfern in 1948 and continued across the city of Sydney until the early 1970s, sometimes replacing terrace housing with high-rise buildings. At this time there seemed to be little awareness of alternative approaches to demolition, such as rehabilitation and improvement of housing. The result was a physical solution focussed on bricks and mortar rather than community, with the underlying assumption that alterations to the physical environment would lead to social and economic improvement for the poor (Coleman 1985).

Queensland

In developing a different role, from its inception the Queensland Housing Authority utilised CSHA funding to a much greater degree than other housing authorities, to develop home ownership programs that constructed homes to sell to homeowners on generous terms (Hayward 1996). The housing that remained unsold was utilised for public rental. Given this emphasis on home ownership, public housing tended to be scattered among private housing developments where it was easier to sell, rather than the situation in New South Wales where it was concentrated in public housing estates (Jones 1972). However, some estates were still constructed as a cost-effective way of building public housing. The focus on home ownership was at the cost of expanding the numbers of public rental stock and Queensland has been consistently characterised by lower public housing stock numbers than other Australian states.

South Australia

The SAHT differed from other housing authorities, in that its role went beyond the provision of rental housing for low-income earners. It innovatively utilised public housing as a way to attract industry and employment to the state by providing low cost rental housing for workers and their families located close to industry. The broader state government agenda was to maintain land and housing prices at a reasonable level. This action provided an incentive for industrial and economic expansion of South Australia by facilitating lower wages and costs for industry.

Hence, much of the post-war public housing stock built in the 1940s and 1950s was on large housing estates surrounding industrial areas. Despite being a signatory to the 1945 CSHA, the South Australian Government maintained independence from the Commonwealth until 1953, by funding housing construction from its general borrowings rather than under the CSHA. Commonwealth loans were seen as having too many conditions attached to the acceptance of funding (Marsden 1986). This situation eventually, in subsequent decades, led to greater problems of debt reduction than were experienced in other states. Nevertheless, the SAHT successfully built up a large supply of stock and promoted the state's economic growth, especially in the era from 1938 to 1965 under Thomas Playford as Liberal and Country Party Premier of South Australia (Stutchbury 1986: 62). Overall, these diverse directions resulted in South Australia constructing the highest proportion of public housing of all Australian states, much of it concentrated on public housing estates. At its peak in the 1960s, social housing in South Australia represented 18% of the total occupied dwellings, more than twice the national average (ABS 1966 in Hayward 1996).

Constructing South Australian public housing estates and social mix

The Salisbury North estate represented the first SAHT development in the northern region of the city of Adelaide. It was constructed from 1950 to 1955 on an area of 160 hectares, 21 kilometres from the central business district, and consisted of 1080 double rental units. The double units, as shown in Figure 1, are a unique characteristic of public housing in South Australia and consist of two semi-detached duplexes divided by a shared common wall on either side. They were designed to house two families, one living on either side, and were typified by large backyards that represented the then conventional standard for family living.

When the estate was initially constructed, the idea of social mix was not considered. At that stage, the SAHT catered mainly to working tenants with families and the imperative was to provide stable, affordable decent housing for the working classes as a stepping-stone to home ownership. Typical of the approach of the SAHT at that time, the housing was used to attract and service the growth in manufacturing industry in the northern regions. The Long Range Weapons Research Establishment (LRWE) located in the immediate vicinity provided a large number of permanent jobs for residents of the estate. Around 75% of the original allocations of housing at Salisbury North went to employees of the LRWE and its allied companies, many of whom were British immigrants (Marsden 1986). This action ensured that the residents were not only of similar class and social mix but also culturally uniform in customs and outlook. Until recently, the SAHT had an open access policy, with no income restrictions, and to this effect eligibility for

Figure 1: Double unit housing at Salisbury North. (Source: Photo originally published in Arthurson K (2008))

public housing rental was simply a matter of applying for assistance and then waiting until a suitable property became available.

Integrating public and private housing

Clearly, when the Salisbury North estate was originally constructed, social mix was not a consideration. The estate was homogeneous in terms of lacking different housing styles and a range of residents across different housing tenures, characterised as it was by low-income working class families in public rental with most families originating from Britain. By the early 1960s these aspects of the estate categorised it through the eyes of outsiders as different, compared with the adjacent private residential areas. The estate also had limited facilities compared with other areas in that it lacked shopping, public transport, health services and other community amenities. The Salisbury North estate was described thus:

> *[As] a blot upon the face of the earth, it's dirty and hardly anyone looks after their places ... I suppose the trust do their best but there are some places there that are a positive disgrace. It doesn't give people much encouragement. (Marsden 1986: 273)*

Support for social mix as a planning tool in housing policy sprung in part from these sorts of debates and criticisms about the sameness and lack of diversity both in housing tenure and the socioeconomic mix of residents of the estates.

Seemingly in an attempt to reconcile some of these issues, together with the stigma attracted to such places, the SAHT planned future estates with a housing tenure mix of public rental tenants and private homeowners. This commonly involved locating the rental housing, generally semi-detached double units, in the middle of the estate surrounded by detached single units that were available for private sale. It is interesting to note that in implementing social mix it was not a fine-grained mix like Cadbury's British development of Bournville where the different classes were housed side by side. Rather it was more like the mix that eventuated in Hampstead in London where the different classes were located in the same neighbourhood but were segregated by clustering housing types in particular pockets of the neighbourhood. The SAHT was able to control and implement this type of social mix as it had developed two separate building programs, houses for sale and public rental housing. The rental housing program was kept separate from the homeowner program, enabling financial viability as the proceeds from sales of the latter were used to fund the building of more rental homes.

Cognisance of the idea of social mix was evident in the SAHT's major construction project of the new town of Elizabeth, which was built soon after Salisbury North in 1954. The project aimed to provide a variety of housing types and tenures to attract a cross-section of income groups to the estate. Peel illustrates that in adapting the British model of new town planning to the Australian context many of the inherent paternalistic ideas about the poor and how they should behave were retained. The advocacy of social mix in the planning and building of the suburb assumed that the working class could not build community on their own and needed middle class role models and leadership to assist them. Planning for Elizabeth was based on the notion that tenants in rental housing, following the example of middle class role models, would aspire to become homeowners (Peel 1995). This assumption was embodied in the way the SAHT grouped and segregated pockets of the neighbourhood according to financial status through the use of topography. At Elizabeth, rental housing was located closer to the factories on the plain, whereas the houses for sale were sited further from the factories on the more desirable inclines and elevated areas. The intention was that tenants would gradually 'move up' the social hierarchy and to better housing (on the slopes) without having to leave the neighbourhood. As the then general manager of the SAHT explained, the rental homes were:

> *Not unattractive but very modest, and as they are basically in the industrial areas it is usually found that when the family moves up the social scale the attitude is, 'it is about time we moved somewhere else, to be amongst right-thinking people'. This idea of making sure these rented properties are not mansions does have that effect. It makes sure that these people just do not camp in low-rental houses all their lives. (Jones 1972)*

These insinuations, that the poor required middle class leadership to become good citizens, were similar to the assumptions underlying the models of 19th century British social reformers that linked housing and social mix. To reiterate, from the viewpoint of Octavia Hill, for instance, 'different classes like different people, have separate characters, which are meant to act and react one on the other' (Hill 1877). In both this early representation and the later characterisations at Elizabeth, the working classes were depicted as disorderly and lacking in moral fibre and were seen to have much to gain from the exemplary behaviour of middle class role models.

International critiques of social mix

In the late 1950s and early 1960s, influential academics in Britain and the US began to debate the relevance of social mix policies. One of the foremost arguments at this time for a balanced neighbourhood was providing middle class leadership for working class public housing tenants to inspire them to develop middle class values (Wood 1960 in Gans 1961*a*; Heraud 1968). A leading commentator in these deliberations, American sociologist Herbert Gans (Gans 1961*a*) raised a number of questions about the desirability of creating heterogeneous communities, together with the efficacy of social mix policies and robustness of the underlying ideas used to support its implementation. He argued that while heterogeneity is desirable where local taxation is the main basis for funding local community services, changing social mix is not a substitute for welfare support, education or community-development programs. Gans suggested that if the underlying economic and social inequalities attached to class were addressed then the increased opportunities may naturally lead to greater heterogeneity within neighbourhoods. In addition, he cautioned that forced heterogeneity or varying social mix of the different classes within particular neighbourhoods could in some instances threaten residents' security and cause conflict or disputes between neighbours. For this reason in particular he supported homogeneity at the spatial scale of the block but heterogeneity at the broader neighbourhood level. These debates were highly contentious in the US, given the related arguments of civil rights lawyers that segregation was racially biased and undemocratic and a 1954 ruling, which recognised that segregation in schools was unconstitutional. Nevertheless, based on his evaluation of community studies conducted in the 1950s and 1960s, Gans (1961*a*) concluded that homogeneity, rather than heterogeneity, of background interests, values and class was essential if contact between residents of neighbourhoods was to develop beyond superficial exchanges to something as substantial as friendship. From this particular perspective, the planners' expectations of closeness developing between middle class and poorer neighbours through spatial propinquity were perceived as simplistic and in effect advocating physical determinism:

Homogeneity of characteristics is more important than propinquity. Although propinquity initiates many social relationships and maintains less intensive ones, such as 'being neighbourly', it is not sufficient by itself to create intensive relationships. Friendship requires homogeneity. (Gans 1961a)

Simultaneously, the results of a series of intensive community studies conducted in the UK were released, further invigorating discussions about social mix and class. Young and Willmott (Young and Willmottt 1957; Willmottt and Young 1960), the investigators of these research studies, appeared somewhat ambivalent about social mix. They merely presented the experiences of working class residents in both heterogeneous and homogeneous communities and found evidence that working class residents who moved to more mixed-income communities were made to feel inferior by their middle-income neighbours:

They have to conform – in a typical Woodford Avenue there seems more uniformity of gardens, attitudes and opinions than in an East End 'turning'. (Young and Willmottt 1957: 129)

In the more mixed-income neighbourhood of Woodford Avenue there was clearly discomfit for the working class residents that was associated with the pressure to 'be the right sort of person, have a decently furnished home ... speak with the right accent, [and] be neatly dressed' (Willmottt and Young 1960: 129). Conversely, in 'classless' or 'one class' neighbourhoods, working class respondents reported that there was a certain comfort in the sameness of background and class. Based on the results of their combined studies, Willmott and Young, along with Gans, called for more empirical studies to be conducted to test the propositions associated with social mix policies.

Other critics of social mix policies argued that desegregation weakened working class communities, in effect robbing the poor of their collective political power. From this perspective, the working class collectives and agencies represented important power structures in society that led to social change. Disassembling this power base enabled the state to take ideological control and redirect the working class away from radical or revolutionary action, thus stymieing instead of advancing working class interests and reforms. For the state, working class cooperation was required to provide the compliant labour force necessary for the smooth workings of capitalism (see, for instance, Simon 1974). Many of these foreground debates about social mix in the 1950s and 1960s appeared to bypass Australian policymakers at the national level as they sought to change the mix of tenants entering public housing to deal with criticisms emerging about this housing tenure.

Questioning the value of public housing: targeting and social mix

In Australia, like other Western countries, the 1970s heralded the end of the long post-war period of full employment and strong economic growth. The processes of economic globalisation and industry restructuring, along with economic recession in 1973–74 meant the loss of manufacturing industry jobs in most areas. These outcomes had a disproportionate effect on the public housing estates, especially those in South Australia, which were built to provide a labour force for local manufacturing industries. Around the same time as the negative effects of economic change were impacting on the delivery of public housing, a debate ensued about who should have access to public housing. Nationally, there were criticisms of relatively affluent families who continued to occupy public housing, which was seen to be at the expense of more deserving families. The Commission of Inquiry into Poverty chaired by Henderson in the mid-1970s identified that the most impoverished groups were not residing in public housing but tended to be private rental tenants (Commission of Inquiry into Poverty 1975). To address this situation, the Henderson Inquiry recommended implementation of new forms of income redistribution, such as cash transfers, targeted specifically to the most disadvantaged groups, which varied significantly from the low-income working tenants to whom the housing authorities traditionally responded. Albeit, the suggested initiative was not housing specific, but it would have enabled the housing authorities to charge market rents and recoup their costs. However, instead of adopting the suggested initiative, the findings of the Henderson Inquiry were applied selectively to argue that subsidisation of better off tenants was occurring, while the most impoverished groups were prevented from accessing public housing. The insinuation in these arguments and debates was that undeserving people were accessing public housing and support developed for the proposition that public housing should be targeted only to people with higher needs. Consequently, in 1978 CSHA proposed implementing market level rents to encourage the better off public tenants to move into private rental. The states agreed, as a compromise, to set 'market related' rents (Troy 1997). An unexpected consequence was that in conjunction with economic change this policy direction eventually led to concentrations of higher need tenants within public housing and the raft of present-day problems that are associated with this situation.

At this stage, at the federal government level, alternative arguments about social mix were not discernible. Broadening access to public housing rather than targeting high needs groups, for instance, provides a spontaneous social mix of tenants from across different socioeconomic levels within public housing. This prevents residualisation of the tenure, and assists the housing authorities to recoup their rental and maintenance costs, making the system financially viable. Conversely, the adoption of tighter targeting coupled with economic change in the 1970s saw the beginnings of the mix in public housing narrowing even further to encompass residents experiencing poverty and unemployment. In reaction to the federal government decision to constrict access to public housing, the debates about the importance of developing a broader social mix intensified at the state government level, particularly in South Australia, where the SAHT until recently had a policy of open access to public housing.

Expectations and aspirations for creating social mix in the 1970s

During the 1970s, support for social mix policies in South Australian planning circles flourished, as reflected in practice in the Hackney North redevelopment located just outside the city of Adelaide. Many of the key ideas and influences were imported from the UK. The Australian planning firm Llewelyn-Davies Kinhill, for instance, drew on their experience with creating social mix in Milton Keynes in the UK when later promoting the concept of social mix in Australia (Sarkissian 1975). Ideas about a balanced social mix were embraced as a reaction to the problems arising in homogeneous housing estates and were seen as a planning solution to stop recreating the problems (Stretton 1975). Several interconnected and complementary debates about social mix coexisted. There were two major assumptions about the benefits it could provide: cross-fertilisation of ideas, culture and habits between the classes; and local funding to afford equitable access to a range of quality services within particular disadvantaged neighbourhoods.

Cross-class fertilisation of ideas and habits

A major assumption of the arguments put forward for the benefits of social mix in 1970s Australia was that propinquity would result in the different classes mingling with each other, or at least having some contact in their day-to-day lives. Hugh Stretton, Deputy Chairman of the SAHT in the 1970s, claimed two principal advantages for socially mixed neighbourhoods. First, heterogeneity of residents within neighbourhoods was thought to expose both rich and poor residents to alternative ways of life:

> *Besides taking each other's children to the speed-car track races and the theatre, there are more important rich-and-poor exchanges of ambition, compassion, and the learning and initiative required to use whatever services are in theory offering. From poorer neighbours, affluent children may pick up better politics, mechanical skills and social capacities than their snobbish schools offer them. (Stretton 1975: 97)*

Second, social mix was also thought to confer benefits on less affluent children by exposing them to middle class children attending the same schools, and in doing so broadening their educational experiences. The manifestation of these benefits relied on contact occurring between the classes. In reality, the experiences of residents of the estates often differed to that envisaged, as middle-income residents tried to distance themselves from neighbours of dissimilar social origins and more mixing was found to take place between residents where there was social homogeneity. For instance, in two studies conducted in the 1970s of the SAHT developed new town of Elizabeth, the middle class residents socialised at local clubs, but most of these clubs were not attractive to working class residents (Peel 1995). These contentions built on the findings of international researchers, such as Young and Willmott (1957) and Gans (1961*a*, *b*) in their earlier community studies, who found that homogeneity rather than heterogeneity of backgrounds made mingling between neighbourhood residents more likely to occur.

Social mix and equitable access to a range of services

As highlighted previously, Salisbury North and other estates constructed in the immediate post-war period often lacked essential facilities, such as shops. The SAHT in its subsequent construction of the new town of Elizabeth attempted to overcome these shortcomings as it designed the town centre and provided land for schools, playgrounds, a hospital and kindergarten. At this stage, in addition to achieving goals of integration between homeowners and renters, social mix was viewed as an important tool to increase access for disadvantaged residents to fundamental goods and services. As Dean Lambert, the then specialist advisor at the SAHT on planning policy, explained, this aspiration was based on the rationale that services are not evenly distributed across different neighbourhoods. Thus, local councils with a mix of property tenures, housing values and resident incomes gain a better revenue base through which to provide infrastructure, services and other amenities than neighbourhoods where the poor are concentrated (Lambert 1979). Likewise, as Hugh Stretton, a then reader in History at the University of Adelaide and board member of the housing trust, articulated:

> *Mixed suburbs can distribute municipal services equally to unequal rate-payers, but segregated suburbs make sure the poor get only what they pay for – including, sometimes, the municipal councillors. Segregation usually unequalises people's access to open spaces – to parks, views, well-kept playgrounds and playing fields, sometimes rivers and beaches. (Stretton 1975: 106)*

From both of these perspectives, the social mix of an area provided a basis for allocating services at an average level and was about equitable distribution of public funds across different neighbourhoods. The discourses about social mix were interwoven with government concerns of achieving equity and social justice and programs funded through the taxation system to provide redistribution of goods and services from the better off to the less fortunate members of society.

From 1973 onwards, changes made to the CSHA enabled housing authorities to purchase and renovate established homes. The SAHT began purchasing existing housing across scattered sites that were 'pepper potted' among homeowners, to rehabilitate and rent rather than constructing new public housing estates. Social mix objectives were often pursued in these types of neighbourhoods against the protestations of private residents that the presence of SAHT tenants would lower the status of the areas (Lambert 1979). The SAHT also began to pursue social mix objectives in new urban developments on greenfield sites, involving joint ventures with the private sector, such as the master-planned communities of Golden Grove and Seaford. In these privately constructed developments, public housing was less concentrated and more integrated with private housing than was possible on the public housing estates. Nevertheless, the expectations expressed for social mix policies in these neighbourhoods were analogous to those preceding them as the creation of 'community harmony' was envisaged first and foremost through the planning technique of social mix and by offering opportunities for working class residents to 'improve their standard of living' (Bosman 2003).

By the late 1970s, there was uncritical support for pursuing social mix objectives in South Australian housing policies. Social mix was an undisputed objective of the SAHT's practice and formed part of the state government's social objectives. The South Australian State Labor Party platform had a commitment to 'the desirability of a greater housing and tenure mix' (Cloher and Badcock 1978). At that time, social mix was seen as a basically innocuous if sometimes paternalistic tool of housing policymakers. The practices associated with social mix were grounded in comprehensive planning and building and ideals of achieving equality and fairness. In particular, the pursuit of social mix objectives in housing policy reflected the commitment of South Australian governments in those earlier eras to applying housing and planning policies concerned with the equitable distribution of wealth and other resources to the less advantaged members of society.

Conclusion

This chapter has sought to enhance understanding of some of the different agendas for social mix in 1970s Australia, and South Australia in particular, where the case study neighbourhoods are located. The conceptualisation of social mix in South Australia in the 1970s was inextricably linked with the state government's broader redistributive ideals and social democratic visions. These ideals aimed to achieve equality of opportunity and social justice through broader planning and housing policy and major government programs to redistribute services to the less fortunate members of society. In spite of this redistributive conceptualisation of social mix, a continuing theme in past ideas of social mix was that propinquity between poor and better off residents enabled the poor to become good citizens through the instrument of middle class leadership. By the 1970s, the defining characteristic, which separated the discourses from the earlier Victorian ideas about social mix, class and role modelling, was the steeping in a social democratic discourse. In a practical sense this amounted to the implementation of redistributive government services. This aim anticipated that mixing between residents involved a valuable two-way exchange between the classes rather than the working class merely becoming clones of the middle class, and perhaps reflected wider Australian concerns with egalitarianism.

References

Arthurson K (2001) Achieving social justice in estate regeneration: the impact of physical image construction. *Housing Studies* **16**, 807–826.

Arthurson K (2008) Australian public housing and the diverse histories of social mix. *Journal of Urban History* **34**(3), 484–501.

Bosman C (2003) Homes for everyone. *Journal of Australian Studies* **27**, 131–145.

Cloher DU and Badcock B (1978) Foreword. In *Proceedings of Royal Geographical Society Symposium on Residential Mix.* (Eds DU Cloher and B Badcock) p. 5. Adelaide.

Cole I and Goodchild B (2000) Social mix and the 'balanced community' in British housing policy – a tale of two epochs. *GeoJournal* **51**, 351–360, doi: 10.1023/a:1012049526513.

Coleman AM (1985) *Utopia on Trial: Vision and Reality in Planned Housing.* Hilary Shipman, London.

Commission of Inquiry into Poverty (1975) 'Poverty in Australia: first main report'. *AGPS* **1**.

Darcy M and Randolph B (1999) *Strategic Directions for Housing Assistance, Urban Frontiers Program.* University of Western Sydney, Macarthur, Sydney.

Gans HJ (1961*a*) The balanced community: homogeneity or heterogeneity in residential areas? *Journal of the American Planning Association* **27**, 176–184.

Gans HJ (1961*b*) Planning and social life: friendship and neighbor relations in suburban communities. *Journal of the American Planning Association* **27**, 134–140.

Hayward D (1996) The reluctant landlords? A history of public housing in Australia. *Urban Policy and Research* **14**, 5–35.

Heraud BJ (1968) Social class and the new towns. *Urban Studies* **5**(1), 33–58.

Hill O (1877) *Our Common Land and Other Short Essays.* Macmillan, London.

Jones MA (1972) *Housing and Poverty in Australia.* Melbourne University Press, Melbourne.
Lambert D (1979) Some practical difficulties of implementing social mix. In *Planning Presuppositions: Social Mix, a Useful Tool? Proceedings of Joint CSIRO-AHRC Seminar on Low Income Housing.* (Ed. C Gribbin) pp. 9–18. Australian Housing Research Council Project 86, Division of Building Research, Melbourne.
Marsden S (1986) *Business, Charity and Sentiment. The South Australian Housing Trust 1936–1986.* Wakefield Press, Adelaide.
Mumford L (1938) *The Culture of Cities.* Harcourt Brace and Company, New York.
New South Wales Department of Housing (2001) The History of Public Housing in New South Wales, Sydney, <http://www.housing.nsw.gov.au/>.
Paris C (1985) Housing issues and policy in Australia. *Built Environment* **11**, 97–116.
Peel M (1995) *Good Times, Hard Times. The Past and the Future in Elizabeth.* Melbourne University Press, Melbourne.
Sandercock L (1977) *Cities for Sale.* Melbourne University Press, Melbourne.
Sarkissian W (1975) A peaceful path to real reform? A critical review of the idea of social mix. Master of Town Planning thesis. University of Adelaide, South Australia.
Simon B (1974) *Education and the Labour Movement, 1870–1920.* Lawrence & Wishart, London.
Stretton H (1975) *Ideas for Australian Cities.* Georgian House, Melbourne.
Stutchbury M (1986) State government industrialisation strategies. In *The State as Developer, Public Enterprise in South Australia.* (Ed. K Sheridan) pp. 60–91. Royal Institute of Public Administration in association with Wakefield Press, Adelaide.
Thornbury R (1978) *The Changing Urban School.* pp. 189–202. Education Paperbacks, Methuen, London.
Troy P (1997) Introductory remarks to the forum: the end of public housing. In *The End of Public Housing? A Discussion Forum Organised by the Urban Research Program 25 October 1996.* (Ed. R Coles) pp. ix–xii. Urban Research Program, Australian National University, Canberra.
Willmottt P and Young M (1960) *Family and Class in a London Suburb.* Routledge and Kegan Paul, London.
Young M and Willmottt P (1957) *Family and Kinship in East London.* Routledge and Kegan Paul, London.

4

Twenty-first century debates: social mix, estate regeneration and social exclusion

Introduction

For several decades after the 1970s there seemed indifference towards ideas about social mix in Australia until the late 1990s when the debates were once again reinvigorated. This time represented a critical juncture in housing policy as administrators grappled with solutions for dealing with managing the problems of increasing concentrations of residents experiencing poverty on public housing estates. Even though by this stage housing authorities had largely stopped constructing large-scale estates, the issues related to homogeneity of tenants within this housing tenure escalated. This was the result of a series of policy decisions about financing and targeting of public housing along with wider economic changes that were set in motion in the 1970s and 1980s. In view of these circumstances it is not surprising that policy deliberations once again turned to social mix as part of the solution for dealing with the growing concentrations of disadvantaged populations on public housing estates.

The UK Labour Government (1997–2010) has linked social mix with addressing social exclusion in neighbourhoods of concentrated disadvantage, which provides an important background context for current-day Australian arguments and policy debates about social mix that have also recently adopted a framework of responding to social exclusion. Clearly this focus is expressed in the Australian Federal Government's unfolding of its 'social inclusion agenda' as reflected in the then Federal Minister for Housing's key speech on housing reform delivered in 2009.

> *We need to create more mixed communities where public housing dwellings are part – but not a feature – of the neighbourhood. Mixed communities are more likely to build social capital – the goodwill, shared values, networks, trust and reciprocity that exist in neighbourhoods [and] will be in a stronger position to confront poverty and vulnerability, resolve disputes, and take advantage of new opportunities ... remaining broad acre public housing estates should be renewed to create mixed communities. This is the way of the future. (Plibersek 2009: 26)*

The current interest in social mix is not restricted to the policy communities. There has also been recent renewed international academic interest in social mix and the analogous topics of 'neighbourhood balance' and 'area effects', as reflected in the flurry of articles and special editions of major international journals, including *Housing Studies* (Vol. 17 and Vol. 18), *Housing Policy Debate* (Vol. 9) and *Urban Studies* (Vol. 38).

This chapter considers the question of why there is a re-emergence of interest in social mix policies at the current juncture in time. In addition, are these new conceptualisations of social mix or the remnants of older debates dressed up in new guises? To explore this question, this chapter briefly considers the key housing policy and economic changes that originated in the 1970s and 1980s, which have gradually intensified over time and now come home to roost in terms of posing major challenges for the contemporary administration of public housing. The end results of the changes have coalesced in the 21st century and are signified by increased concentrations of disadvantaged residents experiencing a multiplicity of issues, the unfavourable reputations attached to many public housing estates, limited funding and the physical problems of aging housing stock. The chapter then draws out the contemporary policy and academic debates that are intermingled with discourses of social exclusion and its dichotomous pair social inclusion, in part demonstrating responses to the considerable social and economic change experienced on public housing estates.

The challenges of managing social housing

Funding reductions

From the mid-1980s onwards, despite the growing demand for public housing and the limited capacity of many tenants to pay full rental costs, Commonwealth

Government funding for public housing declined significantly. Between 1989 and 1999, funding under the CSHA decreased by almost 15% and since then has continued to decline (Steering Committee for the Review of Commonwealth/State Service Provision 2000; Hall and Berry 2006). The decision made by the Commonwealth Government in 1983 to deregulate the Australian finance system meant that higher interest rates were payable on the states' commercial borrowings. For states such as South Australia that took out larger loans to finance construction of greater numbers of public housing, their position was made increasingly difficult by higher interest rates, leading to a build-up of debt. Under the 1989 CSHA the Commonwealth ceased providing concessional loans to the states, with lower interest rates than were available commercially, and simultaneously tightened state financial matching requirements to try and maintain overall levels of funding. The effect was a substantial reduction in the amount of funding available for the state housing authorities to expand the housing stock. Increasingly, attention turned to managing the issues arising from the existing stock, especially where it was concentrated on housing estates as the unfunded liabilities of aging and often redundant stock mounted.

Physical problems of aging assets

At the beginning of the 21st century, there were not only the results of ongoing funding cuts to contend with but also the physical problems of aging and poorly designed housing. When most of the housing estates were first constructed in the 1950s and 1960s they raised the standard of housing to higher levels than ever before (Neutze 1977 in Newton and Wulff 1983). However, in the 1970s much of the newer and superior public stock in the best locations was sold for home ownership with the housing that remained often of poorer quality, aging and situated in the least attractive or unpopular estates (Industry Commission 1993). In the 1980s, several reviews (South Australian Parliamentary Public Accounts Committee 1986; House of Representatives 1987; Bell *et al.* 1988) forewarned of the huge financial cost of dealing with the problems of aging public housing stock along with a maintenance backlog from earlier mass construction that was estimated to escalate over the coming decades. Coupled with the declining trend of public investment in infrastructure, the issue of who should pay for maintenance and replacement of public infrastructure, such as public housing, was left unresolved. The Hawke Government's promise in 1983 to double the public housing stock overall in the following decade did not eventuate and was replaced instead by the focus on tighter targeting and the housing authorities having to achieve more with less funding (National Capital Planning Authority 1993).

As forecast by the reviews of the 1980s these problems have indeed intensified with the physical attributes of the aging post-war housing stock contributing to increasing maintenance costs. The housing is generally of a uniform design, often concentrated on estates and consists mainly of three-bedroom houses with sizeable backyards. Due to demographic changes, present-day demand on the waiting list is predominantly for smaller houses for single, one-parent family, or elderly applicants. In some Australian states there are also problems with the design of newer estates constructed as recently as the 1980s on Radburn principles, which are no longer considered appropriate for public housing tenants. Radburn designs result in houses sited 'back-to-front' with backyards facing out onto streets and cul-de-sac pathways, and the front doors accessed from pedestrian walkways and areas of open public space. This design consists of dead-end lanes preventing ready access for police and emergency service vehicles while at the same time providing increased opportunities for concealed crimes and antisocial behaviour. Coupled with funding cuts and the physical problems associated with public housing, the tenants accessing public housing have become more complex and high need than previously.

Residualisation and concentrations of disadvantaged residents

Ongoing adjustments to Australian public housing incorporate progressively tighter restrictions governing access to the tenure, and wider social and economic changes and reductions in funding have transformed the characteristics of public housing residents. In South Australia alone the restructuring and closure of manufacturing industries in the five-year period from 1979 to 1984 resulted in the percentage of SAHT tenants receiving rental rebates increasing from 35% to 64% (Marsden 1986: 387). The suburb of Elizabeth that was constructed by the SAHT in the 1950s and produced a throng of workers for the car industry became 'a place made poor' (Peel 1993: 36). The increasing numbers of unemployed tenants led to a significant decline in rental income for the housing authorities, undermining the financing of public housing. Coupled with this, successive economic recessions in 1973–74 and 1982–83 and the consequential rises in unemployment caused huge increases in the waiting lists for public housing. New applications for public housing in South Australia, for instance, more than doubled over the period from 1979 to 1984 (Marsden 1986: 387). Simultaneously, as housing authorities were confronted with meeting the increased need for public housing they faced the conflicting demands of operating with less revenue.

The tenure has become residualised, as over time it moved from providing housing for families and low-income working tenants with a proportion of tenants paying full rent, to housing for mostly unemployed and complex, high need tenants. This situation has been exacerbated in the present day as successive CSHAs have required public housing agencies to implement ever tighter targeting to respond to growing problems of homelessness, mental illness and addiction problems (Jacobs *et al.* 2011). The effect of this targeting has been a revision of the composition of households in public housing from the working families of earlier eras, bringing to the public housing estates a level of disadvantage that has made housing agencies and others increasingly aware of these areas as 'troubled estates'

(Arthurson and Jacobs 2006). This creates a paradox: on the one hand housing agencies have to implement policies that create the conditions for estate disadvantage, while on the other they have a responsibility to fix these conditions.

The groups currently housed include those with high levels of reliance on social security payments, and with mental health, physical health and other complex needs and issues. One consequence is that this socioeconomic segregation is highly visible in a spatial sense with neighbourhoods characterised by high concentrations of public housing and impoverished residents located adjacent to neighbourhoods of private housing with more affluent residents. Within some public housing neighbourhoods there are also growing problems of crime and antisocial behaviour that have drawn additional negative attention to the areas (Samuels *et al.* 2002; Arthurson and Jacobs 2006).

Reputation and stigma

In tandem with the foregoing issues, recent civic unrest experienced on some public housing estates, including Macquarie Fields, Rosemeadow and Redfern in New South Wales, has drawn the public's attention to this housing tenure in consistently negative ways. From the point of view of many commentators, the physical characteristics of the housing in combination with the social demographics of tenants stigmatise the public housing estates, which are often depicted as repositories for social exclusion and less than desirable places to live. This notion was reflected in a public statement made in the late 1980s by the then director of the New South Wales Department of Housing that the Radburn estates displayed 'every form of social exclusion which could possibly be devised' (Cappie-Wood 1998: 62).

Media portrayals of the housing estates augment the poor reputations, often exaggerating, misrepresenting and embellishing unsupportive representations of the estates. The Parks public housing estate, located north-west of Adelaide, for instance, was depicted as a 'ghetto' in the media. This resulted when the Minister for Housing and Urban Development at that time, John Oswald, announced commencement of The Parks Urban Regeneration Project. In his words, the project was envisaged to reduce the concentration of 'ghetto' type public housing in the area (Minister for Housing Urban Development and Local Government Relations and Minister for Recreation Sport and Racing 1994). Residents of The Parks were incensed, as despite the negative perceptions attached to the neighbourhood by outsiders, many of the residents liked living there (South Australian Housing Trust and Pioneer Projects Australia 1996). Likewise, the Salisbury North public housing estate attracted negative media coverage, both locally and nationally, when the media identified that John Bunting, the main perpetrator of the now infamous 'bodies in the bank vault' serial killings at Snowtown, north of Adelaide, lived in public housing at Salisbury North. The reputation of public housing gained further notoriety when it was revealed that two of the murder victims' bodies were found buried in the backyard of the house. A book written about the crimes questioned whether people like Bunting are 'the product of a failing society; dereliction by the police, social services, welfare agencies and South Australia's housing trust which has placed them in shabby suburbs with little support' (Smith 2006: 1).

The escalation of the issues experienced by residents in contemporary public housing is also reflected in the change of nomenclature from public housing to social housing. Although not specifically referring to this point, the Federal Minister for Housing in a recent speech on housing reform clearly articulated some of the divergent associations attached to the two terms. As she described it, public housing was originally perceived by government as an 'enabler', a way for people to get ahead in life. For many low-income, working families, public housing facilitates a smooth transition to home ownership. Public housing gradually evolved into 'social housing', a term that invokes pejorative images of a housing tenure that forms part of the social security safety net characterised by 'jobless households and jobless neighbourhoods' with 'very few employed adults as role models' and young people 'having an expectation that they will grow up to rely on public housing just as their parents have done' (Plibersek 2009: 4). An alternative perspective is that the term 'social housing' was adopted by many advocates in the sector (particularly in Victoria) in an attempt to avoid the stigma of residualisation associated with public housing by the 1990s. From this viewpoint the term social housing is used to raise awareness that, similar to the situation in Europe, not-for-profit housing is increasingly provided by community sector organisations rather than public agencies. From this alternative standpoint, social housing is considered the universal term and public housing is the pejorative term.

In endeavouring to respond to the multiple issues facing social housing tenure, the housing authorities have implemented neighbourhood regeneration projects in which a key focus is changing social mix on social housing estates to create more mixed-income communities.

Policy responses: estate regeneration, social mix and social exclusion

Estate regeneration

In Australia, the first estate regeneration projects were implemented by the housing authorities in the 1990s. These earlier approaches were limited to improving the physical characteristics of the housing rather than being developed specifically to address the social problems on the estates. Later responses have attempted to extend beyond this aspect to embrace 'whole of government' regeneration projects with the argument that the complexity and interconnected nature of estate residents' problems require solutions that are much broader than changes to physical infrastructure and housing carried out independently of other social concerns. Whole of government models envisage working in collaboration and partnership with a range of government and non-government agencies including but not restricted to the fields of education, health and police to facilitate integrated service delivery at the local neighbourhood level (Arthurson 2003). A major endeavour of most projects is to create a broader housing tenure and socioeconomic mix of residents on the estates. In the section that follows, discussion returns once again to the Salisbury North estate, some 60 years after it was originally constructed, with the purpose of exploring some of the more recent debates emerging about social mix.

Salisbury North estate and social mix 60 years on

It is within the context outlined of social, economic and demographic changes that the Salisbury North estate was selected for a contemporary estate regeneration initiative. Salisbury North, as detailed in Chapter 3, was the first SAHT public housing estate development in the northern region of Adelaide. The neighbourhood was identified as severely disadvantaged in the early 1990s due to the large numbers of residents experiencing problems of social disadvantage, including higher unemployment levels than surrounding areas (Forster 1991). The SAHT and City of Salisbury (the local government council) initiated the Salisbury North urban improvement study in 1997 to identify ways of improving the neighbourhood. This led to the current-day regeneration project that officially commenced in 1998.

While the overall regeneration project incorporates a number of aspects, including physical maintenance, upgrading and renewal, community development projects and small-scale employment initiatives for local residents, one of the principal aims of the project was to achieve a better balance of social mix. In attaining this goal, the concentration of public housing stock is being reduced from 1390 to 500 houses, which represents a drop from 37% of houses in the area to 15% after regeneration processes are finalised (Arthurson 2001). A more balanced social mix is being achieved through demolition, urban infill and replacement of obsolete social housing with newly built private housing to attract more homeowners to the estate. The regeneration project also requires permanent relocation of some public housing tenants to other neighbourhoods. Within the project documentation, improving the trend in homebuyer interest is the major strategy identified to revise the concentrations of public housing tenure and to develop a more balanced social mix (South Australian Housing Trust 1998). Attracting homeowners to the estate is depicted as an essential approach to thin out the socioeconomic indicators of disadvantage and gain a broader mix of desired characteristics. To achieve a better balance of social mix, the public housing concentration is being reduced overall by 59%.

The aspirations linked to changing social mix are also reflected in the discourses of housing authority staff working on the project that connect a more balanced social mix to the processes of creating 'a greater capacity for individuals to be self-sustaining', a 'longer term community' and a more 'diverse caring community' (Arthurson 2002). In part, the expectation is that social disadvantage is being tackled by developing a more balanced social mix. This perspective is clearly articulated by one of the housing officers working on the project:

> *By significantly changing the demographic makeup of those communities we would believe that those communities should become more self-sustaining in the longer term. (Arthurson 2008, p. 497)*

Undoubtedly from this point of view, 'concentration effects' are regarded as major problems on the estates. Communities with a more heterogeneous socioeconomic mix of residents are characterised as instruments to facilitate community regeneration. In short, it is envisaged that the introduction of homeowners will assist in forming new, improved and better functioning communities. Consequently, the way forward to social improvement for tenants who remain in the regeneration area and those relocated to more dispersed public housing, is achieved by coming into contact with an alternative world to that of their existing communities, including exposure to residents with higher levels of employment and education and more stable family life.

These expectations emphasise a consistent theme in the history of social mix, that spatial propinquity with the middle class, in this case symbolised by the presence of homeowners, provides role models for disadvantaged groups. Thus, in the words of another housing officer, 'with social mix some community standards and values rub off' from middle-income to low-income residents (Arthurson 2008). These ideals reflect similar hopes for social mix to those expressed by the reformers of both the earlier Victorian era and in 1970s Australia. Despite the consistency of this theme about spatial propinquity between different classes, an important observation is that contemporary social mix policies are removed from earlier government frameworks of comprehensive provision of social housing, community planning and building, and goals of social equity and social justice. The social democratic redistributive ideals advocating collective solutions to poverty, including government programs to redistribute services and resources to the less fortunate in society, which were dominant in earlier discussions of Australian policies implemented in the 1970s, are not discernible here.

In the current context of reconfiguring existing estates, which encompass reductions in levels of public housing and rationing of access, the beliefs and assumptions underlying social mix are likely to be less benevolent and more malign. This is especially applicable as it is becoming increasingly difficult for public housing authorities to grapple with problems of antisocial behaviour and other management difficulties arising from residualisation of the social housing tenure. The impasse reached in dealing with these types of problems is perhaps best illustrated by the decision taken by the New South Wales Minister for Housing to demolish the Villawood (East Fairfield) public housing estate in the late 1990s. The fundamental argument presented was that the demolition was part of a major new plan to fight 'systemic social and criminal problems' that needed to be urgently addressed (Minister for Urban Affairs and Planning and Minister for Housing 1998: 2). The key assumption was that a lack of social mix within the neighbourhood contributed to or caused these problems as signified by concentrations of residents that were depicted, especially in the media, as choosing to engage in joblessness, crime and violence. What was lacking within these debates was acknowledgement that these issues may originate from wider structural imperatives of economic and industry restructuring and change that results in unemployment and loss of morale. The alternative debates, as expressed in the 1970s, that reordering social mix is not a substitute for addressing underlying social and economic inequalities or the provision of support services, education and community development, were not discernible. Another principal difference between contemporary and earlier debates about social mix is in the linking to estate regeneration approaches within an emerging framework concerned with addressing social exclusion. Once again, as in the original conceptualisation and adoption of social mix policies into Australian housing and planning policies, the UK discourses about social inclusion have been highly influential in the Australian setting.

Linking social mix to social exclusion

When the Blair Labour Government was elected in 1997, the terminology of social exclusion replaced the previous policy emphasis on dealing with 'poverty' as reflected in the establishment of an across-government, multidisciplinary policy-making Social Exclusion Unit. In this context, urban regeneration policy was linked to the creation of 'mixed-income' communities on social housing estates as part of the New Labour focus on tackling the problem of social exclusion. The policy approach espoused the notion that 'communities function best when they contain a broad social mix' (Social Inclusion Unit 2000: 53). Likewise, this linking of social mix policies to regeneration and addressing social exclusion was reflected in the investigations of the Urban Task Force (1999), which was set up to explore both the causes of urban decline and identify some practical solutions to the problems. The final report highlighted the supposed links between creating mixed-tenure housing and enhancing the long-term sustainability of neighbourhoods.

Our system has encouraged the concentration of poverty, need and families with problems, in a residualised social housing sector, as the worst cases move to the top of the list and often end up concentrated in one area. Instead, we need to support the design of neighbourhoods where different types of housing are fully integrated. (Urban Task Force 1999: 66)

The underlying idea that social mix policies are a 'magic bullet', connected to tackling the problems of social exclusion has been expressed subsequently in numerous UK Government policy documents. In proposing changes to planning policy, for instance, the rationale put forward for mixed-tenure neighbourhoods was that 'it is important to create mixed and inclusive communities which offer a choice of housing and lifestyle' (Office of the Deputy Prime Minister 2005: 1). The aspirations attached to the formation of these mixed neighbourhoods ranged from providing 'lifetime communities' to facilitating 'self-help' and creating 'security' for residents. This commitment of the UK Government to creating mixed communities was clearly reflected in a practical sense through implementation of the 'mixed communities initiative'. The initiative commenced in early 2005 and focussed on regenerating existing disadvantaged neighbourhoods across England. It promoted the construction of neighbourhoods with a more sustainable mix of housing tenures and incomes with the justification that concentrations of deprived residents produce negative dynamics known as 'area effects'. The so-called area effects phenomenon refers to the idea that additional disadvantages compound for impoverished residents when they are spatially concentrated with like residents in particular neighbourhoods. In a policy sense, area effects are visualised as constituting a barrier to addressing problems of unemployment, crime, poor environments and poverty reduction. 'A broad social mix is therefore seen as valuable in itself in creating neighbourhood sustainability and beneficial area effects' (Fordham and Cole 2009: 9). The notion of area effects arose from US academic debates about the causes of poverty that mainly originated from the work of William Julius Wilson (Wilson 1987, 1991, 1997) and Charles Murray (Murray 1984, 1994). Their work is considered more fully after exploring the Australian policy experience with the idea of social inclusion.

In supporting a policy emphasis on the terminology of social inclusion, the South Australian State Government established a Social Inclusion Unit in 2002 that in its mandate clearly reflected the transfer of ideas from the UK initiatives. Aligned to this unit was the creation of a Social Inclusion Board that has focussed on addressing the problems of homelessness and families experiencing place-based disadvantage (South Australian SEU Board 2005). A key element of this work is based on implementing a whole of government model of service delivery as part of The Parks neighbourhood renewal, a large-scale public housing estate undergoing extensive regeneration with substantial changes proposed to the social mix of the five neighbourhoods that comprise The Parks.

At a national level in Australia, the newly elected Federal Labor Government (in 2007) also introduced a specific social inclusion agenda informed by the UK approach. The government's principal policy document that outlines its strategy for social inclusion, 'a stronger and fairer Australia', depicts social housing as a key indicator of poverty and social exclusion. To stimulate the Australian economy after the global financial crisis, a federal government nation building and jobs plan was implemented, with expectations that 20 000 new social housing dwellings would be constructed nationally. The funding through this program was contingent on the states implementing a number of reforms including 'reducing concentrations of disadvantage through appropriate redevelopment to create mixed-income communities that improve social inclusion' (Council of Australian Governments 2009: 14). An additional program, the National Rental Affordability Scheme (NRAS), was implemented offering tax and other funding incentives to encourage institutional investment in affordable housing. The new program aimed to avoid the problems of existing social housing, including the concentrations in particular neighbourhoods and the associated stigma and social exclusion of residents. With this task in mind the NRAS targets low- to moderate-income households to support the development of mixed-income communities, with the expected location of the housing in neighbourhoods largely composed of homeowners, close to inner city areas, facilities and employment. In the first five years of the scheme it is proposed that 50 000 houses will be built. However, it is important to note that even with these additional investments in Australian social housing, due to reductions in stock over the past decades, the total amount of public housing is no higher now than it was in the late 1980s (Jacobs *et al.* 2010).

The difficulties experienced on social housing estates, both in Australia and internationally, have provided fertile ground for the re-emergence of arguments about the benefits of social mix policies as housing authorities grapple with finding solutions to the problems. Given these challenges, most of the debates about social mix are currently concerned with breaking up the concentrations of social housing on estates. However, what is unique in the present debates about social mix is the linking to urban regeneration within a policy framework for addressing social exclusion. Part of the impetus for adopting the label of social exclusion and its dichotomous term of social inclusion to tackle disadvantage is an attempt to avoid the pejorative US race-based debate about spatial segregation and the formation of an urban underclass. The prolonged academic debates of Wilson and Murray heightened awareness of these issues.

Academic debates: concentrations of disadvantaged residents and 'area effects'

As highlighted, current deliberations about social mix are a reaction against new forms of spatial class segregation, as were the debates of earlier epochs that arose in response to the social and economic effects of industrial change processes. The work of Wilson (Wilson 1987, 1991, 1997), an American sociologist, instigated a fundamental debate in contemporary urbanism that has informed present-day debates about social mix and its link to social exclusion. He argued that, in neighbourhoods composed of spatial concentrations of large numbers of similarly marginalised people, residents were further disadvantaged through the processes of 'area effects'. The specific empirical focus was poor African American ghetto residents in de-industrialising regions of the US. The critical point to note is that Wilson explicitly defended a structural economic account of the origins of area effects.

'Structural processes' in the context of these deliberations commonly refer to the broader societal determinants of poverty and inequality that are viewed as factors outside individual control. They incorporate the institutions and broader economic and social structures of society, such as the processes of industry restructuring and organisation, and operation of the welfare state. For instance, from this perspective the processes of de-industrialisation and structural economic change, which impacted on some US regions more than others, produced unemployment and spatial segregation of the poor within particular neighbourhoods. The nub of the issue is that as jobs disappeared from particular regions, more mobile middle-income residents left in search of employment elsewhere and poorer residents remained. Wilson (1987, 1991, 1997) posited that the constraints of the resultant spatial concentrations and segregation of the poor led to the production of a new cultural order, which further dispossessed the disadvantaged and resulted in the development of locally acceptable behaviour and norms that deviated from mainstream society. Youth, for example, maturing in environments where only poor and unemployed people remained, lacked support networks and role models to develop skills and confidence required for integration into mainstream society. In this conceptualisation, 'a person's patterns and norms of behaviour tend to be shaped by those with which he or she has the most frequent or sustained contact and interaction' (Wilson 1991: 60). Thus, successful role modelling may simply involve unemployed youth interacting with employed youth within the local neighbourhood. Where communities remained more varied in terms of residents' socioeconomic mix, middle-income residents were thought to act as a social buffer for the underprivileged. They provided sanctions against aberrant behaviour and conventional role models that acted to alleviate the social constraints posed by neighbourhoods where large numbers of residents were disadvantaged.

Wilson's starting point was that it is not possible to understand communities independently of broader interrelated macroeconomic and social processes that create and sustain them. This is the definitive factor distinguishing his concept of area effects from Charles Murray's analyses about an urban underclass. Murray (Murray 1984, 1994) argues that the problems of poor communities derive from a 'culture of poverty' within the community itself, which is sustained through the workings of the welfare state. From this perspective, the welfare state supports feckless behaviour and fosters dependency rather than promoting a work ethic or building individual agency and capacity for change. Individual agency is used to refer to the question of the extent to which disadvantaged individuals' circumstances arise through their own behaviours or lifestyle choices, and the degree to which they are responsible for changing their situations through modifying their behaviour. Murray's thesis spurred a renaissance of argument, especially in the US, about the existence of a cultural 'underclass' where poverty was depicted as caused by the moral and individual personal failings of the disadvantaged groups themselves. At this juncture it is important to note that the work of both Murray and Wilson arose in the US social and political context and as a dispute about deep-rooted experiences of racial discrimination. As such, the arguments are not readily transferable to the Australian milieu, although Murray's perspective in particular has often been reflected in narrative frames drawing on pathological accounts of the causes of poverty for residents of Australian social housing estates.

While Wilson's (1987, 1991, 1997) work on area effects supports the premise that the origins of unemployment in poor communities are largely structural in nature, the ideas linked to this, that social context disadvantages residents and that conditions can be improved through the existence of heterogeneous communities are clearly about the benefits of a balanced social mix. In effect, Wilson has tried to integrate structure and agency approaches to understanding disadvantage. This question of the extent to which individuals who live in poverty are culpable for their own predicament and the degree to which structural factors affect individual capacity is contested in all areas of social policy analysis. Wilson's exposition arose as a challenge to the ideas of Murray (1984), as reflected in their differing emphasis on structural and agency factors as the causes of poverty and disadvantage and thus the balance of responsibilities of individuals and governments in addressing inequality. Both Wilson and Murray's work has stimulated and informed contemporary policy debate about the benefits of adopting regeneration strategies aimed at changing social mix on social housing estates and allied notions about the benefits of middle class role models for the poor. Wilson was a visiting fellow at the UK Centre for the Analysis of Social Exclusion in 1999, where his work has influenced academic conceptualisations of social exclusion. In his recent attempts to understand the processes of social disadvantage without stigmatising the poor, Wilson has increasingly sought to dissociate himself from the debates about the existence of an urban underclass. As an alternative to 'underclass', in the mid-1990s Wilson adopted the term 'ghetto poor', as demonstrated in his publication *When Work Disappears: The World of the New Urban Poor* (Wilson 1997).

Adoption of the term 'social exclusion' in the European and Australian contexts also in part represents an attempt to maintain distance from American debates about the existence of a cultural underclass and the pejorative associations with adopting the term (Levitas 1998: 21). This includes overt implications for policy development that seeks to solve the problems of an urban underclass and support solutions steeped in practices of social engineering. Within contemporary social housing regeneration projects, tensions about the balance of emphasis placed on social exclusion as an outcome of structural economic change processes – such as loss of jobs and casualisation of employment, or as a product of community, individual behaviours and spatial concentration effects – are likely to emerge in strategies adopted by housing authorities to change social mix on estates. In Australia the social exclusion/inclusion agenda is still unfolding, but in the current context there is a danger that debates about social mix will focus on individual behaviour to the detriment of taking account of broader structural processes that impact on poverty and disadvantage.

Conclusion

The management difficulties currently experienced in the administration of social housing have provided a fecund environment for the reinvigoration of social mix policies. In the contemporary policy context, support for social mix policies is based on the premise that the underprivileged are doubly disadvantaged and at risk of social exclusion due to living in neighbourhoods with concentrations of similar individuals, such as on social housing estates. The negative effects are often explained in terms of limited access to opportunities available to broader society, including job networks and role models of appropriate societal behaviours and norms. Certainly, within Australian estate regeneration policy there are major expectations that social mix strategies will assist in creating inclusive, cohesive and sustainable communities. Within this present-day context the debates are not so much couched in planning for social mix, as they were in the building of the new towns in the 1970s, but rather in diversification of housing tenure and socioeconomic mix on existing social housing estates.

A policy conundrum exists in contemporary social housing access policies that are at odds with other policies aimed at begetting a more balanced social mix in areas of high concentrations of social housing. The gradual reversal over time of the eligibility criteria to house those in greatest need means that low-income, working families that were housed in the past are almost assured they will not currently get housed in social housing. This is because their need is not perceived as urgent relative to other groups, including those with substance abuse problems, homelessness, mental health issues and ex-prisoners. However, this situation ensures that there is not a social mix within the social housing tenure, at least in terms of socioeconomic mix.

What appears obvious thus far in this historical exploration of social mix policies is that whether or not social mix policies are harmless or insidious depends in part on the social and political context in which they are situated. There is a danger that in the contemporary context of residualisation of social housing and the emerging problems of antisocial behaviour on housing estates, the call for implementing social mix policies in Australia will draw on earlier Victorian discourses about fear of the poor and their aberrant behaviour. The risk is that policies will be developed that emphasise the need to manage the behaviour of disadvantaged housing tenants by dispersing concentrations of residents at the risk of ignoring wider structural factors that cause inequality. A middle ground must be reached that balances and recognises the critical interaction between broader structural processes and local agency. The next chapter explores some of the unexpected consequences of contemporary social mix policies.

References

Arthurson K (2001) Achieving social justice in estate regeneration: the impact of physical image construction. *Housing Studies* **16**, 807–826.

Arthurson K (2002) Creating inclusive communities through balancing social mix: a critical relationship or tenuous link? *Urban Policy and Research* **20**, 245–261.

Arthurson K (2003) Whole of government models of neighbourhood regeneration: the way forward? *Just Policy* **29**, 26–35.

Arthurson K (2008) Australian public housing and the diverse histories of social mix. *Journal of Urban History* **34**, 484–501.

Arthurson K and Jacobs K (2006) Housing and anti-social behaviour in Australia. In *Housing, Urban Governance and Anti-social Behaviour.* (Ed. J Flint) pp. 259–280. Policy Press, Bristol.

Bell M, Burns P and Crafter S (1988) Financing infrastructure – a view from South Australia. *Urban Policy and Research* **6**, 84–85.

Cappie-Wood A (1998) New South Wales Housing Authority approach to urban renewal. In *Proceedings of the 1998 National Urban Renewal Seminar Revitalising Housing Areas.* (Eds B Badcock and K Harris) pp. 61–63. Australian Housing and Urban Research Institute, Melbourne.

Council of Australian Governments (2009) 'National partnership agreement on the National Building and Jobs Plan: building prosperity for the future and supporting jobs now'. Council of Australian Governments, Canberra.

Fordham G and Cole I (2009) *Delivering Mixed Communities – Learning the Lessons from Existing Programmes.* Sheffield Hallam University, London.

Forster C (1991) 'Areas of multiple disadvantage in Adelaide: final report to the Planning Review'. Adelaide.

Hall J and Berry M (2006) Making housing assistance more efficient: a risk management approach. *Urban Studies* **43**(9), 1581–1604.

House of Representatives (1987) 'Report of the Standing Committee on Transport, Communication and Infrastructure, Constructing and Reconstructing Australia's Public Infrastructure'. AGPS, Canberra.

Industry Commission (1993) 'Industry commission inquiry into public housing'. AGPS, Canberra.

Jacobs K, Arthurson K, Cica N, Greenwood A and Hastings A (2011) 'The stigmatisation of social housing: findings from a panel investigation'. Final report. Australian Housing and Urban Research Institute, Melbourne.

Jacobs K, Atkinson RG, Spinney A, Colic Peisker V, Berry M and Dalton T (2010) 'What future for public housing? A critical analysis'. Australian Housing and Urban Research Institute, Southern Research Centre, <http://eprints.utas.edu.au/9623/>.

Levitas R (1998) *The Inclusive Society? Social Exclusion and New Labour.* Macmillan, London.

Marsden S (1986) *Business, Charity and Sentiment. The South Australian Housing Trust 1936–1986*. Wakefield Press, Adelaide.

Minister for Housing Urban Development and Local Government Relations and Minister for Recreation Sport and Racing (1994) 'The Parks redevelopment, ministerial statement'. 3 November.

Minister for Urban Affairs and Planning and Minister for Housing (1998) 'New era for troubled East Fairfield housing estate'. Sydney.

Murray C (1984) *Losing Ground, American Social Policy 1950–1980.* Basic Books, New York.

Murray C (1994) *Underclass: The Crisis Deepens.* Institute of Economic Affairs, London.

National Capital Planning Authority (1993) 'Restructuring public housing precincts'. Commonwealth Department of Health, Housing, Local Government and Community Services, AGPS, Canberra.

Newton P and Wulff M (1983) State intervention in urban housing and markets: a case study of public housing development and change in Melbourne, 1945–1980. *Urban Policy and Research* **1**, 2–10.

Office of the Deputy Prime Minister (2005) 'Planning for mixed communities – consultation paper'. ODPM Publications, London.

Peel M (1993) A place made poor. *Arena Magazine* December 1993–January 1994, pp. 36–39.

Plibersek T (2009) 'Room for more: boosting providers of social housing'. 19 March. Speech by the Minister for Housing, Tanya Plibersek MP, Sydney Institute, Sydney.

Samuels R, Judd B, O'Brien B and Barton J (2002) 'Linkages between housing, policing and other interventions for crime and harassment reduction in areas with public housing concentrations final report'. Australian Housing and Urban Research Institute, Melbourne.

Smith K (Ed.) (2006) *Review of Killing for Pleasure: The Definitive Story of the Snowtown Serial Murders*. Random House, North Sydney.

Social Inclusion Unit (2000) 'National strategy for neighbourhood renewal: a framework for consultation'. Social Inclusion Unit, London.

South Australian Housing Trust (1998) 'Salisbury North urban improvement – phase 2 study'. Adelaide.

South Australian Housing Trust and Pioneer Projects Australia (1996) 'The Parks urban renewal project investing in people, housing and land'. Adelaide.

South Australian Parliamentary Public Accounts Committee (1986) 'Forty-fourth report, housing asset replacement'. Government Printer, Adelaide.

South Australian SEU Board (2005) 'Overview of the social inclusion agenda'. Adelaide.

Steering Committee for the Review of Commonwealth/State Service Provision (2000) 'Report on government services 2000'. AGPS, Canberra.

Urban Task Force (1999) 'The urban renaissance: final report of the Urban Task Force'. London.

Wilson WJ (1987) *The Truly Disadvantaged: The Inner City, the Underclass, and Public Policy*. The University of Chicago Press, Chicago.

Wilson WJ (1991) Studying inner-city social dislocations: the challenge of public agenda research. *American Sociological Review* **56**, 1.

Wilson WJ (1997) *When Work Disappears: The World of the New Urban Poor*. Alfred A. Knopf, New York.

5

Great expectations and the unexpected consequences of social mix policies

Introduction

Chapter 4 explored the linking of social mix policies to estate regeneration and the more recent emphasis centred within a framework for addressing social exclusion. This chapter investigates the burgeoning academic literature of the 21st century that principally aims to provide an evidence base for policymakers by testing the supposition that rebalancing social mix within disadvantaged neighbourhoods provides a raft of social, economic and behavioural benefits for social housing tenants. In contrast with the avid support within housing and planning policies for balancing social mix, the research findings are ambiguous and, as will be demonstrated, rather than conclusively lending support for the policies, often provide a wary commentary. A large proportion of the UK-wide programs of research on social mix are funded through an endowed charity organisation, the Joseph Rowntree Foundation (JRF). The foundation is a key proponent in UK debates about social mix. This support is based on its origins from the Quaker cocoa magnate Joseph Rowntree who set up the garden village of New Earswick in York in 1904. Rowntree's vision for social mix evolved from the ideas of the Victorian reformers, which were discussed in Chapter 2. He visualised the advancement of 'a balanced community' in practice through proportional allocation of housing within the neighbourhood to a range of essential professionals, such as doctors and teachers, in conjunction with the working classes (Ravetz 2001). Building on its origins, the modern-day foundation takes the view that it 'is fundamentally opposed to estates containing 100% social housing, which have the unfortunate effect of separating and stigmatising those on the lowest incomes and damaging the life-chances of tenants' (Cowans and Sparks 2003: 1).

Contemporary academic research and debates engaging with the topic of social mix, together with those funded through JRF, have explored a number of themes. These include the relationship with stigmatisation of social housing estates and whether thinning out concentrations of social housing tenants and creating more mixed-income communities will diminish the poor reputations of these neighbourhoods. Another evolving concern of much of the academic literature is investigating whether or not social interaction occurs between social housing tenants and homeowners. This focus is not surprising given the underlying rationale for social mix policies that propinquity of middle-income homeowners will provide role models and leadership for social housing tenants and lead to social (class) integration. This ideal has persisted in various forms throughout the history of social mix from the mid-19th century to the present day. This chapter commences by considering the ways in which some of the principal debates about social mix have been constructed in the academic literature from 1990 to 2009. In the second half of the chapter, discussion then turns to some of the more practical and unexpected consequences of the implementation of social mix policies at the local neighbourhood level, which have thus far received limited attention in the policy debates about social mix.

Expectations and evidence for balancing neighbourhood social mix

As discussed thus far, support for contemporary social mix policies is a response to the problems being experienced on social housing estates. Endorsement of these policies is underpinned by the rationale that mixed-tenure housing communities result in a milieu that facilitates positive change for disadvantaged residents. The anticipated outcomes relate mainly to developing more inclusive, caring communities that lead to other advantages, such as contact with role models of people in employment along with expanded labour market networks. The impetus for these benefits to occur is depicted as geographical propinquity between disadvantaged and advantaged residents in local neighbourhoods. This idea that the affluent could be role models for the disadvantaged has been a continuing theme of proponents of social mix from Victorian England to the present day. In many ways the current circumstances on estates appear similar to earlier catalysts that encouraged support for social mix in Victorian England, such as the social and economic upheavals associated with industrial change that concentrated the disadvantaged in particular neighbourhoods and regions of cities. Once again concentrations of the poor are associated with stigma and fear of their potential for collective behaviour when marginalised from mainstream society, which has been reinforced by present-day riots on some estates. The commonality of these debates about the value of a balanced social mix is that the anticipated goals for social mix are reliant on at least some social contact occurring between different socioeconomic groups. In contemporary debates, this is between homeowners and renters. The research community has become enmeshed in the challenge of trying to assess the validity of these and related arguments. Numerous studies have explored whether social interaction actually occurs between residents across different housing tenures. One common theme examines the factors that may prevent or encourage interaction to take place, such as housing design or children attending local neighbourhood schools. Another theme surrounds whether, in reality, mixed-tenure neighbourhoods lead to the anticipated cohesive and socially integrated communities. A third theme explores the effects of implementing a balanced social mix on the issues of stigma and poor reputations experienced in particular neighbourhoods.

Homeowners as role models, social cohesion and questions about social interaction between housing tenure groups

Love thy neighbour

A common theme of international studies of mixed-tenure housing estates is that, despite living in close proximity to each other, homeowners and social housing tenants inhabit different societal worlds. This makes the likelihood of more than peripheral contact occurring between residents in different housing tenures implausible. The explanations given are that, even where only small income differences exist between owners and renters, homeowners commonly leave the estates to go to work, and participate in various social and recreational activities outside their local neighbourhoods. In contrast, social housing tenants often lack access to motor vehicles and employment and tend to spend additional time on the estates and develop more locally based social networks (Atkinson and Kintrea 2000; Atkinson and Kintrea 2004). In numerous case studies of mixed-income housing developments in the US and UK, it was concluded that there is little evidence that social mix impacts on social interaction and social networks (Schwartz and Tajbakhsh 2001; Camina and Wood 2009), even where lower and higher income residents lived in the same building (Brophy and Smith 1997). Contact that occurred generally involved casual interaction, and was limited to particular locations, such as playgrounds and hallways, volunteer activities and between residents across only a modest range of incomes (Rosenbaum *et al.* 1998).

The probability of interaction occurring appeared even more remote where larger income gaps existed between residents in different housing tenures (Smith 2002). In several reviews of the existing literature it was concluded that, based on the limited evidence available, social housing tenants appear unlikely to interact with other residents in ways that would lead to the anticipated social benefits of social mix (Smith 2002; Kleinhans 2004; Holmes 2006). While friendships did not appear to develop between residents across different housing tenures, residents described their relationships with others in the neighbourhood as 'civil' and 'polite'. Consequently, no evidence was found of role modelling effects in relation to employment or the expected raising of aspirations for social housing tenants owing to the presence of middle-income neighbours (Holmes 2006; Joseph *et al.* 2007).

Housing design, mixing and social integration

A debate has emerged in the academic literature about the effects of the spatial scale of social mix implementation and variations in housing design on the probability of social interaction occurring between neighbourhood residents. Like other studies, these are also concerned with informing policymakers in their practices about the benefits or not of pepper potting, whereby social housing tenants are intermixed with homeowners, versus concentrating social housing tenants in clusters in particular areas or streets within the wider neighbourhood. There are numerous possibilities for consideration. Estate designs may range from different housing tenures in the same block of flats, or with social housing tenants located in houses in different parts of the estates, to rental tenants pepper potted among homeowners, or a mix of rental and owned flats or houses on the same estate but separated from each other.

Not surprisingly, the studies identify that spatial separation of homeowners from social housing tenants undermines opportunities for social housing tenants to interact with their better off neighbours. In effect, in this situation social housing tenants are spatially isolated from other residents, so little mixing between tenure groups or diverse social backgrounds is facilitated (Page and Broughton 1997; Briggs 1998; Jupp 1999; Camina and Wood 2009). In studies where street level mixing of different housing tenures existed, higher levels of cross-tenure contact occurred between residents. Nevertheless, the fact that owners and renters regarded each other as 'ordinary people' and were civil and polite to each other did not result in cross-tenure social networks (Allen *et al.* 2005). It was concluded that the levels of social interaction were quite low and 'hardly sufficient to create a considerably more inclusive society' (Jupp 1999: 45).

Other study findings suggest prudence is best in implementing social mix, as a too fine-grained mix raises the potential for conflict rather than social cohesion, especially where differences in socioeconomic characteristics between residents are large. While in some mixed-tenure neighbourhoods owners and renters did not mind living near each other, opposition increased exponentially as proximity between the residents of the different housing tenures increased. The tensions, in part, seemed to be caused by different values and lifestyles (Beekman *et al.* 2001). In another study by Jupp (1999) it was suggested that propinquity does not lead to conflict and for this reason he advocated pepper potting different housing tenures within neighbourhoods. Nevertheless, the extent of the differences in socioeconomic characteristics between homeowners and renters was unclear and they may have been smaller than in other studies. If this were the case, the findings could lend support to the inverse relationship identified in studies by Beekman *et al.* of residents' socioeconomic level, heterogeneity of characteristics and the degree of social interaction.

Clearly some of these arguments about social mix are similar to those of the earlier community studies conducted in the 1950s and 1960s, which identified that:

> *When differences between people are small, residents of an area can develop tolerance toward each other; they can even agree to ignore some important differences that stand in the way of consensus. More extreme population heterogeneity is not likely to have the same result. (Gans 1961a: 178)*

Findings such as this pose a challenge to government proposals that aim to rebuild more socially integrated, cohesive, inclusive and sustainable communities by balancing social mix via introducing middle-income homeowners into social housing estates.

Children's play, schools and cross-tenure mixing

Another theme identified in studies of mixed-tenure neighbourhoods is that stronger friendships appear to develop between the children residing in different housing tenure groups than is likely to occur among adults (Allen *et al.* 2005). Children's play is acknowledged as important in bringing together different income groups, and specifically in some study findings, social interaction was facilitated when homeowners and renters sent their children to the same local schools (Jupp 1999; Atkinson and Kintrea 2000). However, this finding about children is regarded as inconclusive, as other studies find little evidence of social interaction taking place between different housing tenure groups, even when children attend the same schools (Beekman *et al.* 2001; Lees 2008). An insurmountable factor, as highlighted by Stenson and Watt (1999), is that middle-income residents, for a variety of reasons, including judgements they make about the quality of local schools, often choose to send their children to schools outside their immediate mixed-income neighbourhood.

In summary, a key theme of contemporary academic debates about social mix is the question of whether or not social interaction takes place between residents across different housing tenures in mixed-tenure neighbourhoods. There seems to be some consensus in the debates that meaningful levels of mixing and social interrelations leading to the anticipated benefits of social mix are impractically idealistic. Where social interaction does occur, similar to the community studies of social mix conducted in the 1950s and 1960s, it is usually between residents with similar socioeconomic characteristics.

Neighbourhood reputation, stigma and social mix

Another theme within the academic literature explores the contemporary debate that links social housing concentrations to poor reputation and stigmatisation of particular neighbourhoods. Within these debates, the reputation of a neighbourhood is identified as an important characteristic that may have notable effects on individual residents' opportunities, experiences and social inclusion. The range of pertinent factors mentioned in the literature includes access to employment and educational opportunities and the shaping of residents' social networks and reactionary behaviours (Atkinson and Kintrea 2001). This section starts by outlining some of the pernicious effects for residents of living in neighbourhoods with poor reputations that have been identified in various studies. Then, some of the arguments about whether changing social mix improves neighbourhood reputation are examined.

The effects of living in a stigmatised neighbourhood

A stigmatised neighbourhood is seen to affect residents' access to employment, as some employers, for instance, discriminate against potential employees residing in neighbourhoods with poor reputations on the basis of 'postcode' (Bradbury and Chalmers 2003; Palmer *et al.* 2005; Ziersch and Arthurson 2005). Businesses may be reluctant to locate in or near these stigmatised neighbourhoods, reducing the availability of quality retail outlets and local employers (Atkinson and Kintrea 2001). Other related adverse implications raised in the debates involve substandard local services and amenities, including schools that may have difficulty attracting quality teachers or a diversity of pupils (Galster 2007). A counter argument is that, within some impoverished neighbourhoods, specialised services are often available based on the high concentrations of residents in need, which may not be available if this need falls below a certain service level 'threshold' (Atkinson and Kintrea 2001).

In turn, the perceived reputation of a neighbourhood is an important predictor of residents' intentions to leave the neighbourhood. Findings such as this pose questions about the sustainability of urban renewal policy that artificially creates mixed-tenure neighbourhoods without focusing on enhancing neighbourhood reputation. Those with choice may move out of the neighbourhood leaving only the most disadvantaged residents behind, in effect working against any improvements to neighbourhood reputation (Permentier *et al.* 2009). The reputation of the neighbourhood also undermines the maintenance of the newly created heterogeneous social mix of residents within the neighbourhoods. The remaining residents may then feel trapped in the neighbourhood, adding to the problematic reputation (Kearns and Parkinson 2001).

Related arguments are that the experience of living in an ill-reputed neighbourhood may cause residents to adopt self-defeating behaviours. From this perspective, educational horizons and personal ambitions may be curtailed by fatalistic values linked to place of residence and the effects of experiencing spatially concentrated disadvantage or what some argue constitutes a culture of poverty. Murray (1994), for instance, argues that a 'culture of poverty' is promoted through the workings of the welfare state, in this instance through the development of concentrations of homogeneous social housing that sustain sameness and facilitate tenant dependency and feckless behaviour rather than building individual agency, aspirations and capacity for change. The end point for adopting this frame of reference is policies that focus largely on changing individual agency and behaviours rather than ameliorating structural inequalities. In emphasising a more structural conceptualisation of the issue of neighbourhood reputation and some of the broader societal determinants of poverty and inequality, MacIntyre and Ellaway (2000: 343) identify the reputation of an area as a separate dimension. Reputation is viewed as one of two 'collective social functionings and practices' that are 'socially patterned' but nonetheless impact on the availability of material or infrastructure resources. Within this framework they conceptualise these latter features as 'opportunity structures'. By opportunity structures they refer to the features of the physical and social environment, factors that are viewed as outside individual control, which may be 'health enhancing or health damaging'. From this viewpoint, the way that residents, policymakers and the business sector perceive the reputation of a neighbourhood has potential impacts on opportunity structures and the behaviours of residents. The reputation of the neighbourhood affects the self-esteem and morale of the residents, the available infrastructure and who is likely to move into or out of the neighbourhood. There are some pertinent examples of how collective social functionings and practices around the reputation of a neighbourhood impact in a practical sense on the day-to-day lives of residents. Hastings (2009) found, for instance, that workers may vary the quality of services provided to residents, depending on their perception of the reputation and subsequent merit of the neighbourhood, suggesting that stigma has detrimental consequences for people's lives.

A related literature is also developing that specifically explores the effects of experiencing neighbourhood stigma on residents' health and wellbeing (Palmer *et al.* 2004; Palmer *et al.* 2005; Warr 2005). Sensing fear of crime (without necessarily being a victim of it) and the negative perceptions of lack of safety that are often associated with stigmatised neighbourhoods are linked to lowered health and wellbeing outcomes for residents (Ziersch and Baum 2004; Warr 2005). Interconnected with these debates is the proposition that the perception of control that residents have over the processes of experiencing stigmatisation is an important factor impacting on health and wellbeing (Marmot and Wilkinson 2001). In neighbourhoods with poor reputations, harsh judgements are made about residents, including depictions about the receipt of welfare by an 'undeserving poor' (Palmer *et al.* 2005; Warr 2005). Residents often have little control over these processes, and the resultant feelings of shame, blame, devaluation and depictions of deviating from 'normal' are interrelated with suffering the health-related effects of stigma, including decreased morale and self-esteem and increased anxiety levels (Scrambler 2009). The feelings associated with the occurrence of stigma are likened by some to the experience of racial prejudice and may have analogous detrimental effects on health (Krieger *et al.* 2005; Kelaher *et al.* 2008). In totality, in current debates, the experiences of residents living in neighbourhoods with poor reputations that are viewed as 'dysfunctional' places are thought to doubly reinforce many of the difficulties of already socially excluded individuals and their ability to reach their full potential and become socially included.

The association of social housing neighbourhoods with stigma and poor reputations has important damaging ramifications not only for social housing tenants but also for other eligible individuals and families experiencing housing affordability problems. Recent social surveys undertaken in Australia by Burke *et al.* (2005) report that as many as 46% of Australian households living in private rental accommodation and in receipt of Commonwealth rental assistance[1] claim they would never consider applying for public housing because of its poor reputation.

Changing social mix and neighbourhood reputation

Some studies suggest that increasing the balance of homeowners in areas of concentrated social housing through renewal projects enhances the reputation of the whole neighbourhood (Atkinson and Kintrea 2000; Beekman *et al.* 2001; Martin and Watkinson 2005). A synthesis of the findings from seven studies sponsored by Joseph Rowntree (Holmes 2006) similarly found that increasing tenure mix improved the desirability of social housing neighbourhoods, in particular by enabling existing residents to distance themselves from the prejudice commonly experienced in areas of concentrated social housing. Conversely, Hiscock (2002) concluded that having a mix of tenures does little to enhance the reputation of social housing areas. She identified that, when compared with residents of concentrated areas of social housing, residents of a mixed-tenure area were more than twice as likely to report area reputation as a problem. Similar results were found in 10 case studies of estates with diversified tenure. Private

1 Commonwealth rental assistance is an income support payment for low income households to assist in meeting their housing costs when renting in the private market.

home ownership was associated with enhanced area reputation but, in turn, owners were more likely to identify problems, such as inappropriate social behaviour, as due to the presence of social housing tenants in the neighbourhood (Beekman *et al.* 2001). Allen *et al.* (2005: 4), in a study of three mixed-tenure developments, found that housing design countered the potential problem of tenure prejudice but concluded that there was little or no evidence that mixed tenures 'affected the reputation of the areas, positively or adversely'. Other investigations suggest that neighbourhood reputation continues to be an issue despite the efforts of housing regeneration and community participation projects (Hastings 2004; Warr 2005). On estates with a long history of poor reputation, despite changes implemented to social mix and other regeneration activities, the problems of stigma seem intractable to change (Hastings and Dean 2003; Robertson *et al.* 2008).

Arguments about reputation and stigma are also drawn from studies of long-established mixed-tenure neighbourhoods, which were purpose-built at commencement to encourage social integration across different housing tenures. These neighbourhoods were planned to create social mix from inception rather than changing and rebalancing the existing mix, as in social housing estate regeneration projects. The developments were at least 20 years old at the time they were studied. In studies of these neighbourhoods, social housing tenants did not identify themselves as stigmatised, principally because the neighbourhoods were not associated with social housing by the wider society. These neighbourhoods were generally considered more desirable than concentrated social housing estates, as residents could avoid the prejudice associated with the latter. While mixed-tenure neighbourhoods appeared to avoid the level of stigma attached by outsiders to more concentrated neighbourhoods of social housing, a more perverse finding was that within these mixed-tenure neighbourhoods homeowners were more likely to associate social housing tenants with problems of antisocial behaviour. In one study, social housing tenants reported that they felt as though they were perceived as different and inferior even though social housing comprised only 8% of the dwellings in the neighbourhood (Ruming *et al.* 2004). Nevertheless, most of the social housing was concentrated in three parts of the neighbourhood. Thus, while mixed-tenure neighbourhoods seem to avoid the wider societal stigma attached to neighbourhoods of concentrated social housing, the stigma may become more targeted at the individual level of social housing tenants. In these mixed-tenure neighbourhoods the stigma of social housing tenure was not eliminated but instead appeared at a different spatial scale.

Few studies have attempted to comprehensively explore the processes of how stigma develops and is connected with social housing. Hastings (2004), drawing on interviews with residents, real estate agents and estate workers, identified two dominant discourses, which she typified as 'normalisers' and 'pathologisers'. Normaliser discourses were often utilised by residents and locally based workers that depicted social housing estate residents as similar to the general population and dissociated themselves from employing individualised behavioural explanations of the causes of problems on estates. They emphasised that difficult residents were a minority and thus located problems in a broader, structural, societal influences context much like the explanations offered by the premises of Wilson (1987, 1991, 1997). Conversely, respondents characterised as pathologisers predominantly lived outside the neighbourhoods, had often not visited them, and duly lacked intimate knowledge and experience of the estates or their residents. Nevertheless, they articulated a behavioural discourse much like that expressed by Murray (1984, 1994) in his culture of poverty thesis. This discourse implicated the behavioural characteristics of residents as the cause of the social and economic difficulties experienced on the estates and suggested that the underprivileged were to blame for their own problems.

In summary, the findings of the research are inconclusive about whether changing social mix contributes to or improves the reputation of a neighbourhood that previously had high concentrations of social housing.

Social mix now and then: new and old arguments

In exploring the history of social mix, two principal interpretations have been identified about the appropriate responses to adopt to address concentrations of disadvantage. In reality, the divisions between the two explanations are not as clear cut or obvious as is presented here, as they often overlap and are interconnected. Both of these interpretations lead to the adoption of divergent policy directions. The first discourse predominantly draws attention to sociocultural factors based on a culture of poverty thesis about the poor needing to change their behaviours and pull themselves up by their bootstraps. This discourse reflects contemporary ideas of social mix about middle-income residents providing role models for their disadvantaged neighbours. The second account is concerned with addressing inequalities through ensuring greater equity by viewing social mix as an enabler for providing spatially concentrated poorer communities with important services and infrastructure to ensure that they are not worse off than more affluent communities. This interpretation about social mix was dominant in the 1970s discourses that middle-income homeowners were more likely to demand and successfully attract additional services to the community, such as better-resourced schools. In turn, it was expected that disadvantaged residents would also reap the benefits. In current debates, ideas about social mix supporting a wider taxation base in the local neighbourhood to support the redistribution of services from the wealthier to poorer communities are no longer discernible.

An example of the implementation of this latter type of policy was the building of The Parks Community Centre in South Australia in 1979. The centre was built based on redistributive principles that involved providing increased services to a neighbourhood characterised by low-income residents to raise their living standards and integrate them more fully in the broader community. The services included: a secondary school, childcare facilities, a swimming pool, library, gym, theatre, and health, dental, legal, youth and welfare services. At that time, community integration of social housing residents with the wider neighbourhood was to be achieved through provision of a community complex that not only acted as a focal point where residents could access essential services but also facilitated contact across different levels of the community (Healy and Parkin 1980). In Australia, the introduction of social housing regeneration projects focussed on social mix policies has happened alongside a period of concerted withdrawal and rationalisation of government-funded services. This reduction in services has reversed much of the original community development approach taken by government some 30 years before. As the estate regeneration project commenced at The Parks, for instance, decisions were made that closed the secondary school, computing centre, technical and further education college, family and community services offices, skillshare office and childcare centre.

The closure of the secondary school provided a telling example of the impact of service withdrawal on the local community and showed how such decisions act to worsen rather than lessen the social exclusion of residents. The Parks High School catered for specific needs not met in mainstream education, including incorporating youth with significant behavioural problems. According to the youth worker based at The Parks, the school dropout rate after the closure was around 40% because many of the previous students could not cope with mainstream schooling. The decision to close the school was interpreted in teaching communities as 'a narrowing of the criteria of who is considered as worthy of schooling, [and] an abolition of the commitment to social justice' (Thomson 1999: 39). Hence, in this instance, the secondary school played an important role in social integration through education that was not taken into account by those making the decision to close it. Similar issues have been raised in evaluations undertaken of other regeneration projects (e.g. Rosewood, Mitchell Park) also in South Australia. Residents queried the withdrawal of both public and commercial services from the neighbourhoods over time. As with the high school at The Parks, these services, prior to their removal, acted as focal points where neighbours and others in the local community interacted, providing a sense of community and thereby reducing social exclusion (Social Policy Research Group 1998*a*, *b*) and working towards some of the broader integration aims that are now attached to rebalancing social mix.

A different perspective: some perverse consequences of social mix policies

Internationally, a large amount of energy and resources has been expended trying to uncover the evidence that social mix policies work. Less attention has been given to exploring or analysing some of its 'likely adverse effects' (Bond *et al.* 2010) or more objectionable consequences:

> *In the 'zeal to push dispersal' the focus has been on the logic of concentration versus deconcentration with little focus on the messiness in practice and that this provides a different perspective. (Imbroscio 2008: 114)*

A reason for this lacuna may be that the voices of the disadvantaged themselves (whom social mix policies are meant to assist) are not dominant in contemporary debates, which often ignore the lived experiences of residents. In one US study that did ask residents of mixed-income developments about their views on social mix, they responded that they found the idea insulting, especially insinuation that they were child-like and somehow incompetent at organising their own lives (Rosenbaum *et al.* 1998). The community studies conducted in the 1950s showed how complex the issues are from residents' perspectives and that their views may be at odds with policymakers, leading to unexpected and unintended consequences in implementing policies (Gans 1961*a*, *b*).

Indeed, a focus on implementation in Australia reveals some unpleasant consequences of social mix policies in practice, which could benefit from further investigation, both for the impoverished social housing communities and others on the waiting lists for social housing. To date, four principal questions have arisen about the impacts derived from varying social mix on the social housing estates through regeneration projects. First, what are the consequences for the ongoing supply of social housing stock? Second, what effects do the policies have on existing estate communities? Third, which communities are the policies actually targeted to assist? And finally, what are the impacts of the changes on the problems of antisocial behaviour and other difficulties in neighbourhoods?

Impacts on the supply of social housing

The principal means to change social mix in estate regeneration projects is through demolition of social housing, and the selling of existing unimproved, refurbished or newly built housing mainly through the private market to attract homeowners into the regeneration neighbourhoods. These sales of social housing reduce the overall supply or availability in several ways. In South Australian estate regeneration projects, for instance, for every 3.5 sales of social housing, approximately enough funding to purchase one new replacement dwelling is made (Spiller Gibbons Swan Pty Ltd 1999: 20). Given the disproportionate cost ratio between sales of social housing and purchasing of replacements, large-scale regeneration projects that involve sizeable reductions in social housing to balance social mix within the regeneration neighbourhood result in considerably lower levels of social housing. Table 1 indicates the extent of the scale of the reductions in social housing for some of the major regeneration projects that involve changes to

Table 1: Public housing concentration and stock numbers before and after regeneration on Australian social housing estates

	Concentration of public housing			
Name of project	Before (%)	After (%)	Before (number)	After (number)
Inala (Qld)	52	20	2500	n/a
Manoora (Qld)	90	20–50	555	n/a
Villawood (NSW)	100	0	253	0
Waterloo (NSW)	68.3	68.3	2500	n/a
The Parks (Westwood SA)	60	25	2460*	760
Salisbury North (SA)	37	15	1390	500

Source: Table adapted from one originally published in Arthurson K (2004).
* Figure does not include 500 properties already upgraded prior to regeneration commencing. The Villawood (East Fairfield) estate was demolished and totally replaced by private housing.

social mix around Australia. At Salisbury North, for instance, the planned overall reduction in social housing was from 1390 before regeneration commenced to 500 houses at the end of the project.

These large-scale reductions in concentrations of social housing within Australian regeneration neighbourhoods necessitate permanent relocation of substantial numbers of existing tenants and comes at a significant cost to prospective tenants on waiting lists. The rehousing of tenants suppresses housing allocations in the local region and increases average waiting list times for social housing. The Parks regeneration project alone, for instance, demanded that around 10% of social housing allocations in South Australia were quarantined for tenants relocated from the neighbourhoods due to regeneration (Department of Housing and Urban Development 1996). The social housing waiting list in South Australia in 2009 comprised 20 889 individuals and families (Housing SA 2009). Taken as a whole, social mix policies aimed at regeneration will make it much harder in the future for many socioeconomically disadvantaged people on waiting lists to gain access to social housing.

The consequences for existing communities

A contradiction exists in creating new socially mixed communities, as it involves breaking up or dispersing any existing sense of community in neighbourhoods. The implementation of social mix policies assumes that high concentrations of social housing and cohesive or inclusive communities are mutually exclusive features. In reality, while the situation no doubt varies across Australian estates, housing authority staff that responded to a survey at The Parks and Salisbury North in South Australia and Manoora and Inala in Queensland consistently identified that within particular sectors of the community, notably among long-term residents, a strong and positive sense of community already existed prior to the instigation of changes to social mix (Arthurson 2002).

These findings, that neighbourhoods composed of concentrations of impoverished residents do not necessarily lack social cohesion and active social support networks, are by no means novel (Tesoriero 2003; Clampet-Lundquist 2010). This feature has been acknowledged for a long time as illustrated in the explorations of the earlier seminal studies of disadvantaged communities conducted in the UK in the 1950s and 1960s. In their famous study of *Family and Kinship in East London*, Young and Wilmott (1957) argued that homogeneity of class supported the maintenance of kinship networks, in which adult children lived in the same neighbourhoods as parents.

> *In such a district community spirit does not have to be fostered, it is already there. If the authorities regard that spirit as worth preserving, they will not uproot more people, but build the new houses around the social groups to which they already belong. (Young and Willmott 1957: 166)*

Likewise, a theme of some of the more recent international studies of social mix suggests that social housing tenants relocated as part of tenure diversification projects, in which they are inter-dispersed among homeowners, often maintain networks and social ties in their old neighbourhoods rather than forging new links with their middle-income neighbours (Briggs 1998; Popkin *et al.* 2002). Thus, a key tension exists in the housing authorities' policies to change social mix in regeneration projects in that their actions break up the existing communities to create new communities consisting of different types of residents, housing tenure and socioeconomic mix. The SAHT, for instance, recognised this quandary at the commencement of The Parks Urban Regeneration Project where it was recorded that although the existing residents were characterised by low disposable incomes and concentrated social housing tenure:

> *The area displays much of the traditional closeness and resilience of working class communities ... a degree of innovation and self sufficiency has also emerged as an element of life in the area, often matched with a cooperative approach between neighbours. (South Australian Housing Trust 1995: 146, 147)*

Other studies identified that a significant proportion of elderly residents in The Parks relied on these cooperative social support networks to get by in their day-to-day lives (Spiller Gibbons Swan Pty Ltd 1999). It is interesting to note that the high concentration of public housing in The Parks prior to regeneration did not detract from the popularity of the neighbourhood from the point of view of applicants waiting to access social housing. Around 55% of applicants nominated The Parks as their first preference for housing allocation (South Australian Housing Trust 1995). Ironically, as SAHT staff working on The Parks project identified, after implementing changes to social mix it then becomes necessary to try and recreate community cohesion through integration of new incoming residents 'into existing communities ... [and] the old community and new communities' formed through regeneration (Arthurson 2002).

These sorts of tensions are also apparent in other projects to change social mix where, due to well established social networks, ties and attachments, the longer-term residents are often the most reluctant to relocate to alternative neighbourhoods. One of the Queensland Housing Authority staff members working on the Inala regeneration project remarked, for instance, that when tenants have lived in the same neighbourhood for as long 40 years 'the only way they want to leave is in a coffin' (Arthurson 2002). To some extent it appears possible to ameliorate disruptions to pre-established social and support networks through carefully relocating tenants in close proximity to each other so they can maintain contacts with old neighbours who may remain living on the regeneration site. In some projects where these pre-existing networks were identified, neighbours were moved simultaneously and resettled next to each other. Sometimes this required the relocation of a whole street of tenants. Needless to say, the logistics of these exercises becomes more difficult as the regeneration projects progress over time and greater numbers of tenants are relocated.

Ensuring continuing access to local services within the regeneration neighbourhood is another issue that arises in these projects. This appears of greater consequence for social housing tenants than other groups, given their generally limited financial resources and minimal levels of car ownership. In some impoverished neighbourhoods, specialised services are available based on the concentrations of homogeneous residents in need that otherwise may not be available if this homogeneity falls below a certain service level 'threshold' (Atkinson and Kintrea 2004; Lees 2008).

In summary, tensions emerge between meeting the social mix objectives for regeneration projects that dismantle existing communities and the related goals to improve community integration and self-reliance. In the circumstances where well established, positive and cohesive community networks already exist, there appear some convincing arguments for retaining these communities rather than undertaking large-scale changes to social mix. These collective support structures need to be taken into account in regeneration policy rather than being undermined, as more often seems the case.

Which community benefits?

Another question that arises is which community benefits from changes to social mix and estate regeneration. Is it the established community or the new community created through regeneration incorporating the incoming homebuyers? The homeowners moving to the area and tenants that move back are the principal recipients of enhancements made to the neighbourhoods, including better quality housing, improved physical environments, such as more open space, and enhanced social and support services. While the new communities created through estate regeneration consist of some of the original social housing tenants, fundamental questions remain unanswered when implementing changes to social mix about the effects for relocated tenants who do not move back to the regeneration area. Reductions in the amount of available social housing mean that the capacity does not exist for all of the original tenants to move back to the neighbourhood after the project is completed. The nub of the issue is whether tenants permanently relocated to other neighbourhoods equally benefit from the rehousing processes of regeneration and are successfully integrated into their new communities or find their social networks and access to services disrupted. Few studies have investigated whether, in fact, relocation and regeneration activities alter service accessibility for social housing tenants. Studies accounting for this factor suggest that the requisite services are often more expensive after relocation and sometimes unavailable (Atkinson and Kintrea 2004). In some situations, levels of health care declined, as it was more difficult for residents to access doctors and hospitals (Ambrose 2000).

There are also issues about the potential for gentrification of some neighbourhoods and the increased affordability issues through the influx of homeowners, which may displace long-term residents. Do social housing tenants benefit from sales of social housing for home ownership in estate regeneration? In reality, without financial assistance or subsidy, purchasing of housing is unlikely to be an option for social housing tenants nationally, as 88% of tenants are receiving rebated rents, indicating that they have low incomes and/or special needs, such as a disability or homelessness (Steering Committee for the Review of Government Service Provision 2010: 16.4–16.23). Data available from an evaluation of one regeneration neighbourhood in South Australia (Hillcrest) found that there has been a 329% increase in prices of the housing over the past decade (Toop Real Estate Group 2009). This meant that fewer social housing tenants could afford to purchase the housing, and indeed only nine of the 350 unrenovated houses placed on the market for sale were purchased by tenants (South Australian Housing Trust Undated).

What about antisocial behaviour and other problems?

Varying the social mix through reducing concentrations of social housing, demolition and the relocation of problem tenants from one neighbourhood to another appears a convoluted means to address the issues experienced by tenants on problematic estates. A common theme of the literature is that dispersing difficult tenants simply moves the array of problems, including antisocial behaviour, crime and unemployment, from one neighbourhood to the next. In these situations, rather than leading to constructive solutions, changes to social mix result in broader social and economic costs to the rest of the community (Carlon and Cars 1991; McGregor and McConnachie 1995; Stubbs and Storer 1996). While varying social mix is viewed by governments as an approach for creating socially inclusive communities, it also represents a retreat from using redistributive public policy as a way to alleviate problems of social inequality. Starting from the basis that 'concentration effects' are the main problems that require solving has led to solutions couched in terms of the need to dismantle neighbourhoods through permanently relocating tenants to other areas, rather than dealing with the actual problems of poverty (Peel 1993; Darcy 2007). From this perspective, community is portrayed as the locus of social change and the responsibility is firmly placed on communities themselves through anticipated but highly questionable normalising effects of middle-income role models. Dispersing social housing tenants is also advantageous as a political tool because it deflects attention away from crime, high unemployment, poverty and other social problems experienced by a particular sector of the population. Once the heterogeneous communities are created, the problems of social housing tenants are less noticeable, as in effect, particularly from the perspective of policymakers, the demographic poverty indicators are changed for the better. In reality though, the situation is paradoxical because disadvantaged social housing tenants still exist but they are rendered less visible through dispersal. There are also indications that social housing tenants are 'cherry picked' to ensure that those that remain in the new heterogeneous community are the less problematic tenants, and other objectionable tenants are relocated elsewhere (Holmes 2006).

To date, there has been little consideration of these negative effects arising from the practice of changing social mix. Nevertheless, if the debates concentrated on the pernicious effects of social mix rather than the anticipated benefits, we would need to question what is actually being gained and whether dispersal of social housing tenants and community regeneration are complimentary or intrinsically incongruous policies. The possibility also exists that there are some positive advantages in maintaining certain concentrations of social housing. At the very least, where disadvantage is concentrated and noticeable, it follows that concerted government action is obligatory, although, arguably, the right sort of actions have not always been adopted. The alternative to concentrations of disadvantaged tenants might be worse. When they are dispersed, rendered invisible or isolated in a new mixed-income community, it could easily become a case of 'out of sight, out of mind'. More work needs to be done on investigating social housing tenants' access to services after regeneration and following up relocated tenants in longitudinal studies to see how they fare. There has been limited follow-up research in Australia on whether relocated tenants fare better, or if the problems of crime and disorder re-emerge along with certain difficult individuals transferred to adjacent neighbourhoods (Baker and Arthurson 2007).

Alternative approaches to manufacturing social mix

Given the potential inadvertent and negative impacts of changing social mix identified here, how much emphasis should be placed on balancing social mix as a component of addressing concentrations of disadvantaged social housing residents? We have no way of knowing, for instance, if a community with 80% social housing will function any better than one with 50%, or indeed 20% social housing. Alternatives to balancing social mix are possible, such as targeting regeneration activities to existing residents to compensate for the lack of social and economic resources in the neighbourhood or having policies that allow broader access to social housing.

Targeting activities to integrate existing communities

An alternative approach to changing social mix is to recognise poverty and disadvantage as key issues and focus on community development approaches that build stability and integration in existing communities to render the neighbourhoods more desirable places to live. This sort of approach seeks to compensate the existing community for the lack of material and economic resources that are available in the neighbourhood. An example of a contemporary renewal project that encompassed such an approach was the Waterloo regeneration project in NSW. It was built on this philosophy and differed from other regeneration projects in that changing social mix on the estates was not an aim of regeneration. The project utilised a joint partnership between the NSW Department of Housing, the University of NSW School of Social Work and local residents. While the objectives of the project reflected similar aims to other projects around Australia, to attain an 'empowered', 'self-sustainable' and 'cohesive' community (Arthurson 2002), the directions adopted to achieve these goals differed. All of the regeneration activities were targeted at existing residents *in situ* whether it was employment strategies, improvements to the amenities of the high-rise housing, increased community services or projects to reinforce the sense of ethnic diversity. The ideal was to make the estate a more desirable place to live for current residents.

In taking this perspective, poverty and the lack of material resources for residents of the social housing estates were depicted as key factors undermining a lack of social inclusion of residents in activities of mainstream society, more so than not residing among or next door to middle-income homeowners. The project's aims were built on the idea that poverty prevents many social housing residents from accessing activities that others in society take for granted, such as recreational pursuits (University of New South Wales School of Social Work 1998). The breadth of individual project activities was broad, one example was the community gardens project, which is still operating and has attracted visitors from other neighbourhoods and won awards for the residents. In addition to increasing internal community cohesion between residents, this sort of activity generated positive publicity for the estate (University of New South Wales School of Social Work 1999).

The composition of the Waterloo community did not change substantially throughout the renewal activities because the concentration and level of social housing during the life of the project remained constant at around 68.3% (New South Wales Department of Housing 1998). Consequently, the Waterloo project, unlike other renewal projects, did not involve reductions to social housing or permanent relocation of tenants to other neighbourhoods. Thus, at Waterloo there is no question of which community the range of renewal activities benefitted.

Broadening social housing allocation policies

The inherent tensions existing between social mix policies and current social housing access policies that are targeted at the most complex, high need and difficult tenants require careful consideration. An alternative option to creating social mix through changing housing tenure in urban renewal is to implement less stringent access criteria for social housing, to vary the socioeconomic mix of residents. Historically, there are persuasive arguments about the benefits of allowing broader access to services to meet the government's social justice objectives, although they are not dominant in contemporary debates about social mix. Some proponents, for instance, argue that taking this approach is the only way to counteract the unwillingness of middle-income taxpayers to support the disadvantaged and the associated stigma (Castles 1990). This was the approach originally utilised by the SAHT, which up until recently had an open access policy of admitting anyone who did not own property. The benefits of this model were that higher-income working tenants paying full rent subsidised lower-income tenants receiving concessional rents. The system maintained viability through generating income for basic administration and maintenance, and the stigma associated with the tenure was circumvented.

The policy direction opted for tighter targeting, which has shifted social housing to a last resort where only tenants fitting special needs criteria or in dire circumstances are eligible for assistance. If this direction continues, future communities on estates will be characterised by even greater poverty and disadvantage and more difficult tenants, making the estates harder to manage for social housing organisations. In turn, this situation may be a deterrent to private homeowners. Arguably, what is required to resolve these issues is alternative perspectives to dominant contemporary thinking about the necessity for targeting social housing to increasingly higher need and more complex groups.

In the US over past decades, realisation of the problems around administering and sustaining a residualised social housing sector has seen a revision of previous policies that targeted social housing only to the most impoverished. The *Quality Housing and Works Responsibility Act 1998* required all new housing developments to comprise mixed-income tenants. In this model of social housing provision, 40% of housing is targeted to the 'poorest of the poor' tenants and 60% to working poor to middle-income families (Editor 1998). It is also acknowledged that this creates an income mix within the social housing tenure and avoids concentration of impoverished residents, while at the same time providing an income stream to cross-subsidise more disadvantaged tenants.

Conclusion

In this chapter, the key debates in the academic literature about social mix were explored. In the 1960s and 1970s, the majority of academic debates were concerned with critiquing, evaluating and posing questions about the actual desirability of creating mixed-income communities. In contemporary discourses, however, there appears to be less energy and insight directed at this aspect, or indeed the unexpected consequences of social mix policies. Instead, there appears to be more acceptance that, at least for policymakers, social mix is 'an established orthodoxy' (Wood 2003: 47) so the way forward is to unravel the evidence for its expected benefits. Another omission is the voices of the disadvantaged themselves, which are not dominant in contemporary debates, nor were they in historical debates.

Of principal interest in the debates was the idea that mixing different housing tenure groups provided middle-income role models for disadvantaged members of communities, purportedly increasing their aspirations. Academics have been engaged in unravelling the evidence or otherwise for this anticipated benefit of social mix. This ideal is identifiable as a consistent historical argument that has predominated in the debates of different groups supporting social mix from the past through to the present day. Albeit, in contemporary debates the discourses more specifically refer to housing tenure as a proxy term for socioeconomic class rather than referring to class *per se*.

A new contemporary debate is linked to the concentrations of social housing tenure and the idea that changing the social mix will improve the reputation and stigma of these types of neighbourhoods. Verification of this belief remains inconclusive, although some studies indicate that improvements to neighbourhood reputation may occur through the introduction of homeowners into neighbourhoods of concentrated social housing. However, as discussed, the findings vary about the overall effects on the reputations of social housing neighbourhoods of increasing the balance of homeowners in areas of concentrated social housing.

From a different perspective, a number of perverse consequences of social mix policies were identified that raised questions about whether the policies work against social inclusion for disadvantaged residents. These factors include reductions in overall numbers of social housing stock and the loss of the benefits it provides in term of affordability and security of tenure compared with private rental. Existing communities that may have long-term ties and connections between residents are disrupted and the policies result in dislocation of communities. Another issue is that in viewing concentration as the problem rather than poverty it seems that policymakers are just moving the problems of disadvantage and antisocial behaviour from one neighbourhood to another. As highlighted elsewhere, an unemployed person is of major cost to the community whether they live in one neighbourhood or another (Stubbs and Storer 1996).

An alternative option for Australian social housing to be sustainable involves increasing the housing stock and widening rather than narrowing the eligibility criteria to attract less impoverished tenants. From this perspective, the problems associated with a lack of heterogeneity in social housing are related to better off households not being eligible to access social housing and the limited stock available to support a broader mix of tenants. The exploration in this chapter also highlighted a key tension between housing authorities' social mix policies that attempt to recreate social mix on social housing estates while simultaneously implementing tighter access to social housing. In tandem, the policies have contradictory purposes.

Overall, the research findings about the utility of creating social mix are inconclusive and thus academic discourses on the whole have provided a cautious commentary that contrasts with the enthusiastic support adopted for the policies by housing and planning policymakers.

References

Allen M, Camina M, Casey R, Coward S and Wood M (2005) *Mixed Tenure, Twenty Years On – Nothing Out of the Ordinary.* Joseph Rowntree Foundation, York.

Ambrose P (2000) 'A drop in the ocean. The health gain from the central Stepney SRB in the context of national health inequalities'. Health and Social Policy Research Centre, University of Brighton.

Arthurson K (2002) Creating inclusive communities through balancing social mix: a critical relationship or tenuous link? *Urban Policy and Research* **20**, 245–261.

Arthurson K (2004) Conceptualising social inclusion in estate regeneration policy: what part does public housing play? *Just Policy* No. 34, 3–13.

Atkinson A and Kintrea K (2000) Owner occupation, social mix and neighbourhood impacts. *Policy & Politics* **28**, 93–108.

Atkinson R and Kintrea K (2001) Disentangling area effects: evidence from deprived and non-deprived neighbourhoods. *Urban Studies* **38**, 2277–2298.

Atkinson R and Kintrea K (2004) Opportunities and despair, it's all in there. *Sociology* **38**, 437–455.

Baker E and Arthurson K (2007) Housing, place or social networks: what's more important for relocating tenants? *Australian Planner* **44**(4), 28–34.

Beekman T, Lyons F and Scott J (2001) 'Improving the understanding of the influence of owner occupiers in mixed tenure neighbourhoods'. ODS Ltd for Scottish Homes, Edinburgh.

Bond L, Sautkina E and Kearns A (2010) Mixed messages about mixed tenures: do reviews tell the real story? *Housing Studies* **26**(1), 69–94.

Bradbury B and Chalmers J (2003) 'Housing, location and employment'. Australian Housing and Urban Research Institute, Melbourne.

Briggs XD (1998) Brown kids in white suburbs: housing mobility and the many faces of social capital. *Housing Policy Debate* **9**, 177–221.

Brophy P and Smith R (1997) Mixed income housing factors for success. *CityScape* **3**, 3–32.

Burke T, Neske C and Ralston L (2005) 'Which households eligible for public housing do not apply and why?' Australian Housing and Urban Research Institute, Melbourne.

Camina M and Wood M (2009) Parallel lives: towards a greater understanding of what mixed communities can offer. *Urban Studies* **46**(2), 459–480.

Carlon G and Cars G (1991) Renewal of large-scale post-war housing estates in Sweden: effects and efficiency. In *Neighbourhood Regeneration: An International Evaluation*. (Eds R Alterman and G Cars) pp. 130–146. Mansell Publishing, London.

Castles F (1990) Middle-class-welfare by the back door? *Australian Society* June, 33–34.

Clampet-Lundquist S (2010) Everyone had your back. *Social Ties, Perceived Safety, and Public Housing Relocation, City and Community* **9**, 87–108.

Cowans J and Sparks L (2003) *Consultation Response to ODPM on the Planning Policy Guidance Note 3: Housing – Influencing the Size, Type and Affordability of Housing*. Joseph Rowntree Foundation, York.

Darcy M (2007) Place and disadvantage: the need for reflexive epistemology in spatial social science. *Urban Policy and Research* **25**, 347–361.

Department of Housing and Urban Development (1996) 'South Australian Housing Assistance Plan 1995–1996'. Adelaide.

Editor (1998) Editor's introduction. Don't end it, blend it: are mixed-income housing projects good social policy? *Housing Policy Debate* **9**, 699–701.

Galster G (2007) Neighbourhood social mix as a goal of housing policy: a theoretical analysis. *International Journal of Housing Policy* **7**, 19–43.

Gans HJ (1961*a*) The balanced community: homogeneity or heterogeneity in residential areas? *Journal of the American Planning Association* **27**, 176–184.

Gans HJ (1961*b*) Planning and social life: friendship and neighbor relations in suburban communities. *Journal of the American Planning Association* **27**, 134–140.
Hastings A (2004) Stigma and social housing estates: beyond pathological explanations. *Journal of Housing and the Built Environment* **19**, 233–254, doi: 10.1007/s10901-004-0723-y.
Hastings A (2009) Poor neighbourhoods and poor services: evidence on the 'rationing' of environmental service provision to deprived neighbourhoods. *Urban Studies* **46**(13), 2907–2927.
Hastings A and Dean J (2003) Challenging images: tackling stigma through estate regeneration. *Policy & Politics* **31**, 171–184.
Healy J and Parkin A (1980) *The Parks Community Centre: An Evaluative History.* Flinders University of South Australia, Adelaide.
Hiscock R (2002) 'Mixing tenures: is it good for social well being?' Paper presented at the European Network for Housing Research Conference, Vienna, 1–5 July 2002.
Holmes C (2006) *Mixed Communities, Success and Sustainability.* Joseph Rowntree Foundation, York.
Housing SA (2009) 'Housing in focus, 2007–2008'. Department of Families and Communities, Adelaide.
Imbroscio D (2008) '[U]nited and actuated by some common impulse of passion': challenging the dispersal consensus in American housing policy research. *Journal of Urban Affairs* **30**, 111–130, doi: 10.1111/j.1467-9906.2008.00381.x.
Joseph M, Chaskin R and Webber H (2007) The theoretical basis for addressing poverty through mixed income development. *Urban Affairs Review* **42**(3), 369–409.
Jupp B (1999) *Living Together: Community Life on Mixed Housing Estates.* Demos, London.
Kearns A and Parkinson M (2001) The significance of neighbourhood. *Urban Studies* **38**, 2103–2110.
Kelaher M, Paul S, Lambert H, Ahmad W and Davey Smith G (2008) The impact of different measures of socioeconomic position on the relationship between ethnicity and health. *Annals of Epidemiology* **18**, 351–356.
Kleinhans R (2004) Social implications of housing diversification in urban renewal: a review of recent literature. *Journal of Housing and the Built Environment* **19**, 367–390, doi: 10.1007/s10901-004-3041-5.
Krieger N, Smith K, Naishadham D, Hartman C and Barbeau E (2005) Experiences of discrimination: validity and reliability of a self-report measure for population health research on racism and health. *Social Science and Medicine* **61**, 576–596.
Lees L (2008) Gentrification and social mixing: towards an inclusive urban renaissance? *Urban Studies* **45**, 2449–2470.

MacIntyre S and Ellaway A (2000) Ecological approaches: the rediscovery of the role of the physical and social environment. In *Social Epidemiology.* (Eds L Berkman and I Kawachi) pp. 332–348. Oxford University Press, Oxford.

Marmot M and Wilkinson RG (2001) Psychosocial and material pathways in the relation between income and health: a response to Lynch *et al. British Medical Journal* **322**, 1233–1236.

Martin G and Watkinson J (2005) *Rebalancing Communities by Mixing Tenures on Social Housing Estates.* Joseph Rowntree Foundation, York.

McGregor A and McConnachie M (1995) Social exclusion, urban regeneration and economic reintegration. *Urban Studies* **32**, 1587–1601.

Murray C (1984) *Losing Ground: American Social Policy 1950–1980.* Basic Books, New York.

Murray C (1994) *Underclass: The Crisis Deepens.* Institute of Economic Affairs, London.

New South Wales Department of Housing (1998) 'Draft Waterloo neighbourhood improvement program plan for 1998/99'. New South Wales Department of Housing Central Sydney Region, Sydney.

Page D and Broughton R (1997) *Improving the Design and Management of Mixed Tenure Estates in London.* Notting Hill Home Ownership, London.

Palmer C, Ziersch A, Arthurson K and Baum F (2004) Challenging the stigma of public housing: preliminary findings from a qualitative study in South Australia. *Urban Policy and Research* **22**, 411–426.

Palmer C, Ziersch A, Arthurson K and Baum F (2005) Danger lurks around every corner: fear of crime and its impact on opportunities for social interaction in stigmatised Australian suburbs. *Urban Policy and Research* **23**, 393–411.

Peel M (1993) A place made poor. *Arena Magazine* December 1993–January 1994, 36–39.

Permentier M, Van Ham M and Bolt G (2009) Neighbourhood reputation and the intention to leave the neighbourhood. *Environment and Planning* **A41**, 2162–2180.

Popkin S, Harris J and Cunningham M (2002) 'Families in transition: a qualitative analysis of the MTO experience: final report'. US Department of Housing and Urban Development, Washington, DC.

Ravetz A (2001) *Council Housing and Culture: The History of a Social Experiment.* Routledge, London.

Robertson D, Smyth J and McIntosh I (2008) *Neighbourhood Identity: Effects of Time, Location and Social Class.* Joseph Rowntree Foundation, York.

Rosenbaum J, Stroh L and Flynn C (1998) Lark Parc Place: a study of mixed-income housing. *Housing Policy Debate* **9**, 703–740.

Ruming KJ, Mee KJ and McGuirk PM (2004) Questioning the rhetoric of social mix: courteous community or hidden hostility? *Australian Geographical Studies* **42**, 234–248, doi: 10.1111/j.1467-8470.2004.00275.x.

Schwartz A and Tajbakhsh K (2001) 'Mixed income housing as social policy: the case for diminished expectations'. Paper presented at the 43rd annual conference of the Association of Collegiate Schools of Planning, Cleveland, OH, November 8.

Scrambler G (2009) Health-related stigma. *Sociology of Health and Illness* **31**, 441–455.

Smith A (2002) *Mixed-income Housing Developments: Promise and Reality*. Joint Center for Housing Studies of Harvard University and Neighbourhood Reinvestment Corporation, Cambridge, MA.

Social Policy Research Group (1998*a*) 'Community Perceptions of Social Outcomes of Urban Renewal in Mitchell Park'. Report prepared for the SAHT, University of South Australia, Adelaide.

Social Policy Research Group (1998*b*) 'Community Perceptions of Social Outcomes of Urban Renewal in Rosewood'. Report prepared for the SAHT, University of South Australia, Adelaide.

South Australian Housing Trust (1995) 'The Parks urban renewal project, community development and social impact strategy.' Adelaide.

South Australian Housing Trust (Undated) 'Hillcrest project completion report'. Adelaide.

Spiller Gibbons Swan Pty Ltd (1999) 'Public housing estate renewal in Australia'. Australian Housing Research Fund, Sydney.

Steering Committee for the Review of Government Service Provision (2010) 'Report on Government services 2010, part G, housing'. Productivity Commission, Canberra.

Stenson K and Watt P (1999) Crime, risk and governance in a southern English village. In *Crime and Conflict in the Countryside*. (Eds G Dingwall and S Moody) pp. 76–93. University of Wales Press, Cardiff.

Stubbs J and Storer L (1996) 'Social cost benefit analysis of the NSW Department of Housing's Neighbourhood Improvement Program, case study: Airds'. NSW Department of Housing South Western Sydney Region, Sydney.

Tesoriero F (2003) Housing renewal in The Parks community, South Australia. In *Community Practices in Australia*. (Eds W Weeks, J Dixon and L Hoatson) pp. 74–79. Pearson Education, Frenchs Forest, NSW.

Thomson P (1999) That's where my house is. Arena Magazine 42, August–September, 37–40.

Toop Real Estate Group (2009) 'Boom headlines for property … some very big numbers thrown around this week', <http://adelaide-real-estate-news.blogspot.com/2009_06_01_archive.html>.

University of New South Wales School of Social Work (1998) *Waterloo–Redfern Community Development Project*. University of New South Wales, Sydney.

University of New South Wales School of Social Work (1999) *The Waterloo–Redfern Community Development Project (WRCDP), New and Ongoing Projects*. University of New South Wales, Sydney.

Warr DJ (2005) Social networks in a discredited neighbourhood. *Journal of Sociology* **41**, 285–308.

Wilson WJ (1987) *The Truly Disadvantaged: The Inner City, the Underclass, and Public Policy.* The University of Chicago Press, Chicago.

Wilson WJ (1991) Studying inner-city social dislocations: the challenge of public agenda research. *American Sociological Review* **56**, 1–14.

Wilson WJ (1997) *When Work Disappears.* Alfred A. Knopf, New York.

Wood M (2003) A balancing act? Tenure diversification in Australia and the UK. *Urban Policy and Research* **21**, 45–56.

Young M and Willmott P (1957) *Family and Kinship in East London.* Routledge and Kegan Paul, London.

Ziersch A and Arthurson K (2005) Social networks in public and community housing: the impact on employment outcomes. *Urban Policy and Research* **23**, 429–445.

Ziersch A and Baum FE (2004) Involvement in civil society groups: is it good for your health? *Journal of Epidemiology and Community Health* **58**, 493–500.

6

Mixed-tenure neighbourhoods reconstituted

Introduction

Before reporting on the findings of the present study, in Chapters 7 and 8, about residents' perspectives about social mix, this chapter introduces the three neighbourhoods investigated for the current study. A brief background context is provided for each of the neighbourhoods, then in the final section the data collection method utilised for the study is outlined.

Three reconstituted socially mixed neighbourhoods

The three neighbourhoods utilised as case studies were all constructed by the SAHT in the post-war period in the 1950s and are located within the metropolitan region of Adelaide. Some of the principal comparative characteristics of the neighbourhoods prior to the urban renewal project are summarised in Table 2.

These neighbourhoods were targeted by the SAHT for urban renewal on account of the aging, low-density social housing in poor physical condition along with a growing concentration of residents experiencing socioeconomic disadvantage. The social housing was sited on large parcels of land with big backyards, often one-quarter of an acre blocks. This aspect reflected the standards of the time, when the housing was developed to cater for working families with children. In the present day, such large backyards are underutilised, and

Table 2: Summary of the characteristics of neighbourhoods selected for urban renewal

Urban renewal project	Distance from CBD	Main reason site selected for urban renewal	Project start date	Type of housing	Social housing mix/ concentration of social housing	
					Before	After
Mitchell Park	10 km south	Poor quality housing and cracking in foundations	1986	Semi-detached double units	75% n = 1000	35% n = 350
Hillcrest	8.5 km north-east	Increasing age and poor condition of housing and concentrations of residents with social problems	1994	Timber-framed imported dwellings	60% n = 350	10.2% n = 118
Northfield	10.3 km north-east	Increasing age and poor condition of housing, concentrations of residents with social problems and availability of land for new housing	1991	Semi-detached double units	27% n = 226	19.9% n = 238

Source: Phillips 1994; South Australian Housing Trust 2005; City of Port Adelaide Enfield 2010*a*, 2010*b*.

considered unsuitable for the single parent families, people living alone and elderly tenants that increasingly comprise the waiting lists for social housing. Initially, the large land holdings provided an opportunity to increase housing density in large-scale regeneration projects to fund social housing upgrades through trade-offs made with private sector partners and building of new homes. The next section outlines a brief background history of the development and specific characteristics of each of the three case study neighbourhoods.

Mitchell Park

Mitchell Park is located 10 kilometres south of the city of Adelaide in South Australia. The original settlements in the area extended along the local Sturt River banks, which were used for farming, such as vineyards, market gardens and orchards. As the requirement for land around Adelaide grew after the Second World War, the area of Mitchell Park was utilised for housing development. In particular, large-scale migration programs from the UK increased the demands for housing in the metropolitan region of Adelaide. The Chrysler car plant established in 1955 (that later became the Mitsubishi assembly factory) provided employment for many of the local residents until its closure in 2008. Over the years, key amenities and services developed in the local area, including the Tonsley Park Railway Station, the Westfield Shopping Centre with cinemas and department stores, public and private schools and hospitals, and Flinders University.

The Mitchell Park urban renewal project commenced in 1986 and was completed in 2005. It was the first of the SAHT's attempts at urban renewal. At its commencement, the primary project area contained around 1000 dwellings, of which the SAHT owned 75% or approximately 750 dwellings (Table 2). Eighty-five per cent of the social housing was in the form of the original double units. The initial project focussed on demolishing 60 of the double units. This direction was adopted in order to build new housing on the site, and also to address the structural problems of the existing housing. Many of the houses were experiencing cracking due to the reactive soil type that was a characteristic of the area and inadequate footings provided when the houses were first constructed. Initially, the Mitchell Park renewal project increased the density of social housing in the overall neighbourhood to around 80%, and 100% in the project area. This was achieved through demolition, urban infill of new social housing and subdivision of large backyards.

Based on its experiences, in 1991 the SAHT decided to revise its approach to urban renewal. Instead of continuing to increase the concentration of social housing in the neighbourhoods through demolition and urban infill they turned their attention to diversifying the social mix. This change in direction reflected recognition that there were other issues to contend with beyond the age, physical condition and high maintenance requirements of the old housing. The SAHT registered that tenants were increasingly characterised by low-income, often single parent families and blue collar workers affected by industry restructuring and subsequent high levels of unemployment. By 1995, for instance, unemployment at Mitchell Park was 16% compared with an average of 12% in metropolitan Adelaide. In addition, 25% of residents were sole parent families, 57% were on low incomes and 25% had no access to a motor vehicle (Proctor 1995; SA Better Cities 11 Steering Committee 1995).

The housing authority perceived that increasing the density of social housing was further concentrating the problems of social disadvantage, unemployment and crime in the neighbourhood. The housing trust officials acknowledged that 'replacing the old double units with new houses was only making Mitchell Park look nice on the outside, while the social problems continued to exist' (Hopkins 1999: 19). In part, the social problems were intensified due to land in the neighbourhood being designated for a transport hub, the Tonsley Park Interchange, which failed to eventuate. Housing was set aside for demolition to make way for the planned interchange until some years later when the proposal was eventually abandoned. In the intervening years the housing was utilised to provide temporary emergency accommodation and little maintenance was completed on it. This meant that the housing became rundown and it also catered for the lowest income groups. These groups included single parents that were continually moved into and out of the neighbourhood, which worked against the facilitation of community stability (Marsden 1986).

Over time, as the social problems in the neighbourhood increased, the perception intensified that concentrating disadvantaged tenants together had detrimental effects. Concentration of disadvantaged residents began to be recognised as the causal factor of problems that needed to be tackled rather than poverty *per se*. At this stage, social mix policies came to the fore with the idea that 'the reduction in the concentration of SAHT stock and an improvement in the quality and choice of housing and public amenity' were critical factors to ensure successful results for the urban renewal project (South Australian Housing Trust 2005: 3). Eventually, the aim was to substantially reduce the public ownership of housing at Mitchell Park to around 24% but this factor depended on the newly built houses selling successfully on the private market. The role of marketing, planning and managing sales of the housing was carried out by the private sector. The SAHT had joint partnerships with various private firms to construct new housing and upgrade existing dwellings. Revenue to fund the urban renewal project was raised through sales and retention of some housing for social rental. For instance, in a later stage of the renewal project the SAHT had a joint partnership with Hindmarsh Adelaide, who constructed 21 houses. The SAHT retained 10 houses and allowed 11 to be sold (Hoth 2002). Over the 19-year period of the urban renewal project, 456 properties were demolished (out of the original 1000), 642 new properties were built and around 150 properties were renovated and either retained by the SAHT or sold on the private market (South Australian Housing Trust 2005: 3). By 2005 when the project was completed, the percentage of social housing concentration in the neighbourhood had been reduced from the original 75% to around 35% (South Australian Housing Trust 2005).

The midpoint evaluation of the Mitchell Park urban renewal project posed some important questions about the success of the social mix aspects of the project. Specifically, it identified that social housing tenants felt sceptical about whether new incoming and more affluent homeowners really wanted to live next door to them (Social Policy Research Group 1998: 69). This indicated, at least from the perspective of some social housing tenants, that renewal activities aimed at creating more mixed-tenure communities raised awareness of income and class differences, rather than smoothing the way to develop socially integrated communities.

Hillcrest

The Hillcrest urban renewal area is also located close to the central business district, 8.5 kilometres north-east of the city of Adelaide. Hillcrest was officially named as a suburb in 1954 and prior to its development at that time for housing the land was generally used for farming. Before the renewal project commenced, Hillcrest, like Mitchell Park, was recognised as a stigmatised neighbourhood composed of concentrated social housing. However, the Hillcrest urban renewal project was a smaller-scale project than Mitchell Park. As shown in Table 2, the total project area encompassed 350 houses under SAHT ownership.

At Mitchell Park, much of the social housing was characterised by first generation, aging duplex or double units. At Hillcrest, although the housing was of similar age, it largely encompassed three-bedroom, timber-framed, prefabricated and imported housing built on separate allotments. The timber-framed housing was initially favoured for its quick assembly, which enabled the SAHT to meet the high demands for supply in the early 1950s (SA Better Cities 11 Steering Committee 1995). At the time of construction the lightweight housing was also considered ideal for the reactive soil, which caused movement and cracks in sturdier housing foundations. Of course this type of problem was later rectified by advanced technology, such as brick veneer construction on concrete raft footings. Over the years, the condition of the timber-framed houses deteriorated, resulting in higher than expected maintenance costs for the SAHT (Proctor 1995).

In selecting the Hillcrest area for urban renewal in the mid-1990s, in addition to the poor physical condition of the housing the concentration of disadvantaged social housing tenants was identified as a key issue. This was reflected in resident demographics: around 19% were unemployed, 27% were sole parents, 55% had low annual incomes and 22% had no access to a motor vehicle. There was also a perception held by the wider community that crime and violence were higher in the Hillcrest neighbourhood than the surrounding areas (Proctor 1995). The Hillcrest area was stigmatised in part because the Hillcrest Mental Hospital was constructed on the site in 1926, adjacent to 230 hectares of farmland. The farmland supplied the hospital with milk and provided manual work for the patients. This land was utilised from 1958 onwards for the Northfield Research Centre for horticultural research. The more recent policy direction to de-institutionalise the care of people with mental health problems and provide them with services to live in the community resulted in the closure of Hillcrest Mental Hospital in 1992, several years before the urban renewal project commenced. The remaining residents were transferred to the other state government long-term psychiatric institution of Glenside Hospital, located on the eastern side of the city of Adelaide.

The Hillcrest urban renewal project formerly commenced in 1994 with the appointment of the private developer Brock Barrett as project manager. The focus was somewhat different from other urban renewal projects planned by the SAHT in that it formed one of the four precincts that comprised the larger overall Northfield area urban infill project. The whole project encompassed a mix of approaches including infill of backyards with new houses, demolition, refurbishment and replacement of existing social housing stock, private sales and subdivision of land for new housing. The first precinct included the development of Regent Gardens (later renamed Oakden), an urban infill project adjoining the Hillcrest area. This stage of the development involved the building of 1250 new homes on land that was previously owned by the Department of Agriculture. The two adjacent neighbourhoods of Hillcrest and Regent Gardens consisted of quite different socioeconomic groups, with the social mix at Hillcrest mainly comprising social housing tenants compared with a predominance of homeowners at Regent Gardens. A key aim of the renewal project was to ensure that the Hillcrest housing trust area merged with the new private housing at Regent Gardens to encourage integration of public housing tenants and homeowners. This goal was a response, in part, to a survey on the needs of existing Hillcrest residents that highlighted their concerns about the negative image of the Hillcrest area and the high incidence of vandalism and crime (Hazebroek 1992).

The strength of the commitment to social mix policies was reflected in the Hillcrest urban renewal project objectives 'to reduce the concentration of public housing in Hillcrest to approximately 20%' and to 'ensure a mix of public and private housing without concentrations of public housing' (South Australian Housing Trust *et al.* Undated: 3). The project involved removing 350 timber-framed social housing dwellings representing nearly 60% of the total number (580) in the neighbourhood (South Australian Housing Trust Undated) and subdividing the land into 430 allotments consisting of various sizes. Of these allotments, 37 were retained by the SAHT to build new housing. An additional 150 masonry homes were owned privately or by the SAHT. At Hillcrest, the overall density of housing was increased by 30% but the percentage of social housing was eventually reduced from 40% to 6% (Skewes and Taylor 1996). This decision necessitated the relocation of over 300 tenants over a three-year period and sale of housing on the private market to encourage private homeowners into the neighbourhood (South Australian Housing Trust *et al.* Undated: 6). Social housing tenants interviewed before and after relocation from Hillcrest admitted to feeling socially isolated among private homeowners. This situation arose due to class differences becoming more obvious between social housing tenants and other residents than had been evident in the original concentrated areas of social housing at Hillcrest (Ruediger 1998).

A study conducted in the late 1990s sought to evaluate whether or not the integration component of the renewal project between social housing tenants at Hillcrest and private homeowners in the adjoining suburb of Oakden was successful (Biggins and Hassan 1998). It focussed specifically on the residents' acceptance of socioeconomic diversity and the new mix of social and private housing in the neighbourhood. There were significant differences in the distribution of residents' incomes between the two areas. At Hillcrest, 71.2% of respondents had low incomes (<$25 000) compared with only 36.1% of Oakden respondents. Higher approval for the new mixed-tenure housing community was expressed by low-income (79.4% approved) and high-income earners (>$55 000, 65%) than middle-income earners ($35 000–$55 000; 40%) (Biggins and Hassan 1998: 39). Overall, the level of approval from respondents was higher at Hillcrest (71.4%) than at Oakden (67.5%) when income levels were accounted for. The findings seemed to suggest that where social distance was least, that is, from the point of view of middle-income earners, there was greater disapproval of the new mixed-income community. It seems that middle-income residents want to distance themselves from those in the income strata below, which is consistent with general findings on social interactions, social networks, social aspirations and social distancing (Kleinhans 2004; Bretherton and Pleace 2011; Kleit 2011). The present study also found that social housing residents often retained strong ties with friends and family outside the neighbourhoods. Nonetheless, on the whole there appeared to be a fairly high degree of approval for the mix of social and private housing in the two neighbourhoods (Biggins and Hassan 1998: 111). However, not all of the respondents' comments made about the changes were positive. Around 43% of respondents at Hillcrest and 30% at Oakden expressed the view that the way the development was done 'had divided the community along socioeconomic class status lines' (Biggins and Hassan 1998: 28).

Northfield

Northfield is located 10 kilometres north of Adelaide and was subdivided for urban development in 1925. Over the years, large portions of the land were utilised by organisations providing various community and industrial services, including the Hampstead Rehabilitation Centre, Morris Hospital (tuberculosis), Northfield Hospital (infectious diseases), Yatala Labour Prison and the Department of Agriculture. The area has long experienced a poor reputation due to some of the industrial uses of the land. The Northfield Prison for males was built in 1854, prior to the area being developed for housing, but gradually housing was built around it. Initially, the prisoners quarried rock along the local creek for construction purposes and the building of roads. The Northfield Pig Research Unit that opened in 1970 also caused problems due to malodours and issues with the disposal of effluent. The rehabilitation centre opened in 1932 to care for people with infectious diseases, such as polio. It grew rapidly and by 1936 included an administration building, infectious disease block and large laundry operation. In 1978 the centre converted to a 200-bed hospital (Royal Adelaide Hospital 2010).

The Northfield area has been characterised by urban infill, physical renewal of social housing assets and the release of vacant land for new housing developments. The redevelopment of the area was identified more as an urban consolidation initiative than a specific social housing urban renewal project. The now remaining parcel of land that comprises the Northfield area adjoins the suburb of Hillcrest and the new housing development of Walkley Heights. The SAHT originally owned 120 double units and 106 imported dwellings in the neighbourhood, which comprised 27% of the total housing (Table 2). The houses were built on blocks of land that averaged 725 square metres so they provided good potential for subdivision into smaller allotments in a favourable location within 10 kilometres of Adelaide. Like in the other case study neighbourhoods, Mitchell Park and Hillcrest, the overall concentration of social housing in the Northfield neighbourhood has reduced (27% to 19.9% respectively). Conversely, the overall level of social housing at Northfield has increased slightly ($n = 226$ to $n = 238$) (Table 2).

Collecting the data

The data collection for the research involved in-depth interviews conducted with 40 residents across the three neighbourhoods: Mitchell Park, Hillcrest and Northfield. Of these respondents, 16 lived in homes they owned or were paying a mortgage for, 14 lived in social housing and 10 were renting in the private sector. As detailed, these neighbourhoods have been revitalised over the past 15 to 20 years through demolition and sale of social housing, urban infill and new housing for private sale. The interviews canvassed a broad range of topics relating to social mix and its relationship with day-to-day neighbourhood life, focussing specifically on drawing out residents' experiences and perceptions. Each interview lasted for approximately 1 to 1.5 hours. The interviews were tape-recorded and transcribed verbatim, providing a rich source of data on the residents' understandings about a range of topics related to social mix. This included their perceptions about any links between the changes made to social mix and neighbourhood reputation, and the sense of community and social integration of residents. The transcripts were collated by drawing together thematic issues in order to identify patterns, similarities and differences.

Conclusion

This chapter has outlined a short background history of each of the three case study neighbourhoods to provide context for the current study findings. The data collection method utilising in-depth qualitative interviews was also introduced. The following chapters explore the findings of the current study in relation to two of the key expectations held by policymakers for social mix policies: the reputation of socially mixed neighbourhoods; and the sense of community and social integration of residents.

References

Biggins N and Hassan PR (1998) 'Northfield precinct one, a review of the social objectives'. Department of Sociology, Flinders University of South Australia, Adelaide.

Bretherton J and N Pleace (2011) A difficult mix: issues in achieving socioeconomic diversity in deprived UK neighbourhoods. *Urban Studies* in print.

City of Port Adelaide Enfield (2010*a*) 'Profile of Hillcrest, based on the 2001 and 2006 Australian Bureau of Statistics Census of Population and Housing', <www.Portenf.sa.gov.au/webdata/resources/files/Hillcrest1.pdf>.

City of Port Adelaide Enfield (2010*b*) 'Profile of Northfield, based on the 2001 and 2006 Australian Bureau of Statistics Census of Population and Housing', <www.Portenf.sa.gov.au/webdata/resources/files/Northfield1.pdf>.

Hazebroek A (1992) *Northfield Project Community Plan.* Kitchner Press, Adelaide.

Hopkins N (1999) Mitchell Park: surviving urban heart surgery. *Marion City Limits* Spring, 19–20.

Hoth T (2002) An examination of the social and physical outcomes of urban renewal with reference to the Mitchell Park urban renewal project. Bachelor of Urban and Regional Planning thesis. University of South Australia, Adelaide.

Kleinhans R (2004). Social implications of housing diversification in urban renewal: a review of recent literature. *Journal of Housing and the Built Environment* **19**(4), 367–390.

Kleit RG (2011) Integrated or isolated? The impact of public housing redevelopment on social network homophily. *Social Networks* **33**(2), 152–165.

Marsden S (1986) *Business, Charity and Sentiment. The South Australian Housing Trust 1936–1986.* Wakefield Press, Adelaide.

Phillips J (1994) 'Redevelopment strategy'. Policy and Planning Branch, Department of Housing and Urban Development, Adelaide.

Proctor I (1995) 'Priorities for redevelopment'. Correspondance to the Federal Department of Housing and Redevelopment, 23 January.

Royal Adelaide Hospital (2010) 'Hampstead Rehabilitation Centre, a campus of Royal Adelaide Hospital, a history – from then to now', <www.rah.sa.gov.au/hampstead/downloads/HRC_2002-2003_AR.pdf>.

Ruediger M (1998) Social impacts of urban renewal and relocation on Public Housing Tenants in Hillcrest. Honours thesis submitted for Bachelor of Arts in Sociology, School of Social Sciences, Flinders University of South Australia, Adelaide.

SA Better Cities 11 Steering Committee (1995) 'Report of the SA Better Cities 11 Steering Committee northern Adelaide urban renewal study'. Department of Housing and Urban Development, Adelaide.

Skewes A and Taylor M (1996) Community planning for the Northfield project – towards good practice in SA urban projects authority. *Beyond the Fringe* **8**, 10–12.

Social Policy Research Group (1998) 'Community perceptions of social outcomes of urban renewal in Mitchell Park'. University of South Australia, Adelaide.

South Australian Housing Trust (2005) 'Mitchell Park urban renewal project, analysis and determination of the social, physical and financial changes and outcomes in Mitchell Park: study brief'. Adelaide.

South Australian Housing Trust (Undated) 'Hillcrest project completion report'. Adelaide.

South Australian Housing Trust, Brock Barrett and City of Port Adelaide Enfield (Undated) 'Hillcrest renewal project'. The Sales and Information Office, South Australia.

7

Neighbourhood reputation, stigma and social mix

Introduction

As discussed thus far, the justification informing contemporary support for social mix policies is the idea that concentrations of social housing within spatially defined areas generate insidious social and behavioural effects. The policy debates view neighbourhoods with concentrated social housing as a cause of social exclusion for residents; the solutions are then couched in terms of diluting these concentrations to rebalance the social mix. The portrayals of social housing in these debates are almost consistently negative, offering continued support for policy interventions to rebalance social mix and obscuring contrary arguments that demonstrate the 'non-shelter benefits' of social housing accruing to disadvantaged households. These benefits include income related rents and greater housing security than in private rental (Darcy 2009: 10). From the private sector partners' perspective in Australian urban renewal projects, creating a balanced social mix is an obligatory component connected with the marketing and reimaging of the regeneration neighbourhoods. The mandate is to attract new middle-income homebuyers to the neighbourhoods to augment the financial viability of the projects (Arthurson 2001). The media has actively supported and embellished depictions of social housing estates as sites of disorder and crime, citing individual agency and tenants' behaviours rather than poverty as the cause of the problems (Arthurson 2004). The issues are viewed through a lens that explains the difficulties experienced in social housing neighbourhoods mainly in terms of deteriorating social values and the behaviour of tenants rather than structural inequality. Nevertheless, some social housing estates have attracted stigma and poor reputations, whether rightly or wrongly, which do have insidious effects on residents, as delineated in Chapter 6.

Thus, an overall but somewhat understated aim of the three contemporary Australian social housing estate regeneration projects involving changes to social mix was to improve the reputation of the neighbourhoods. The key approaches included building new housing to attract homeowners into the neighbourhoods and permanently relocating many social housing tenants to other neighbourhoods, in effect attempting to rebalance neighbourhood social mix. The success of sales of new private housing to people from outside the neighbourhoods was also, to some extent, contingent on making improvements to neighbourhood reputation.

As highlighted previously, residents' viewpoints have not been accorded precedence in debates about social mix. A great deal of the research is uninformed by residents' experiences, and as a consequence, little is known about the way residents perceive the reputations of their neighbourhoods (Link and Phelan 2001: 365) nor the extent to which the experiences and dynamics of neighbourhood reputation and stigma differ between housing tenure groups (Permentier *et al.* 2009). Throughout history, the middle classes have tended to speak for the disadvantaged as if they know what is best for them, with some exceptions, such as the work of Peel (2003), which enabled people to tell their own stories. With these discrepancies in mind, this chapter utilises the qualitative findings from the in-depth interviews conducted with social housing tenants, homeowners and private renters. Of particular interest was ascertaining how residents across the different housing tenure groups view the issues of social mix and neighbourhood reputation. Do they think, for instance, that social mix helps to reduce stigma? Or are they impartial to the whole idea?

Interview findings

Stigma, social mix and discourses about integration

Many of the respondents remarked that the changes to social mix had assisted in reducing the poor reputation previously associated with their neighbourhood. This perspective appears consistent with other studies that have suggested that socioeconomic mix is a key determinant of neighbourhood reputation, in which homogeneous estates have a more negative reputation than when they were socially mixed (Musterd 2008). In the current study, some respondents from Mitchell Park and Northfield clearly espoused an 'integration' type of discourse about the new social mix in the neighbourhoods. This group included homeowners, and public and private renters. Categorisation of these responses as an integration discourse indicates that positive views were expressed about the mix of different housing tenure groups and, in particular, the influx of homeowners into the neighbourhoods. Respondents suggested that mixing the different housing tenures together had helped to reduce the previous stigma associated with high concentrations of social housing and disadvantaged residents within the neighbourhoods.

> *Well, having known what it was like in the past I'm very proud of my neighbourhood! ... Mitchell Park was a troubled area that had a lot of the crime and drugs, and fairly run-down ... But as many people have said to me now, 'oh my goodness you know you can't even buy into Mitchell Park now it's so popular'. (Social housing tenant MP2)*

> *A lot of people have said Mitchell Park is really good now but when I told them I was moving there they raised their eyebrows 'oh that's a wild area or something like that'. (Homebuyer MP1)*

> *I think it's good. A mix of people I think is always good. I'm in favour of that. (Private renter N204)*

> *I know when we first moved here [in 1973] the police told us it was called the Bronx. (Homebuyer MP45)*

> *I think it's wonderful. I say 'I live at Mitchell Park' and people sort of raise an eyebrow and then suddenly they remember 'ah that's right there's been a huge development going on there hasn't there?' and you say 'yes it's so good, it's like living at Mawson Lakes[1] with all the fancy houses!' (Social housing tenant MP2)*

Residents at Hillcrest adopted a similar 'integration' discourse that was positive about the changes to social mix and linked reduced stigma of the neighbourhood to reductions in concentrations of social housing.

> *Hillcrest 30 years ago was an area that if you lived in Hillcrest you certainly didn't boast about it. (Homeowner H155)*

> *I know that Hillcrest had a really, very bad name many years ago because it was all housing trust. For some reason or other, housing trust people don't seem to have a good name and yet the people that I know here were very nice people. (Homeowner H40)*

> *They [housing trust residents] are all mixed in everywhere but they're not as noticeable now as they used to be. They've blended them in so that you really*

1 Mawson Lakes is a new housing development in Adelaide that this respondent, and many other South Australians, consider a desirable place to live.

don't know which ones are the housing trust homes and which are the bought ones. They've done it that way on purpose I think, so they don't stand out. (Homeowner H98)

However, the responses at Hillcrest differed slightly from the other two case study neighbourhoods. Here, the integration discourse that was expressed by respondents clearly associated the improved reputation of Hillcrest with the urban renewal project and promotion of the adjacent private sector housing development of Oakden:

[Oakden] was a very upmarket sort of sales promotion thing and that. They then started Hillcrest advertising, when they did the redevelopment right next door to Oakden. They attached it to that. You saw it becoming more pleasurable, more likeable, more upmarket as things progressed. (Social housing tenant H35)

If I say I live at Hillcrest they kind of look down their nose, but as soon as I tell them it's on the border of Oakden they go ahh ... because it's trendy and new and modern and more expensive. (Homebuyer H7)

Conversely, at Northfield some residents felt as if their neighbourhood was purposely differentiated and cut off from any association with the adjacent private housing development of Northgate:

I guess the biggest thing I noticed ... all the houses that went up along the strip of the street where Northfield meets Northgate got white picket fences along their front yards so it was like this social division where we are Northgate and we are Northfield and I sort of thought that's not very good is it? I sort of cringed and it's like rubbing it in people's faces about we live in Northgate and you don't. (Private renter N204)

Many of the interviewees generally expressed the view that they were very proud of their regenerated neighbourhoods. Once again, some respondents expressed an integration discourse about the positive benefits of the new mix of housing tenures in the neighbourhoods. Comments were often made that the neighbourhood 'definitely looks nicer', 'certainly has improved' and that the different housing types 'blend in really well'. In addition, residents specifically connected the changes to tenure mix, and the related upgrading of the social housing to make it 'less visible' or detectable as such, with increased feelings of pride in the neighbourhoods stating, for instance that:

The houses that are obviously privately owned and the trust houses that I would imagine that have come into private ownership they all seem to be blending in so well together and taking pride. (Social housing tenant MP2)

I think it's changed. I think it's a lot better now than what it was. (Social housing tenant H2R)

Homeowners also acknowledged broader tenure mix as an important practice to decrease the visibility of social housing. This integration of different housing tenures compared with prior concentrations and segregation of social housing was depicted as an important way to decrease the stigma associated with residing in social housing:

It also allows someone who is reliant on public housing to be that little more invisible and not to be stigmatised by being obviously housed in a housing trust enclave ... It doesn't stigmatise those who simply, possibly because of circumstances are on a low income by being branded housing trust. (Homeowner H155)

Although the new mix of housing tenures was expressed as lowering the stigma for socioeconomically disadvantaged groups living in social housing, the belief was commonly expressed that some outsiders still probably viewed the neighbourhoods negatively, remembering them as they were before. It was recognised that broader public images of the neighbourhoods may take a while to adjust unless they actually visited the neighbourhoods to witness the positive changes first hand:

They think Hillcrest is still old and crusty ... I know most of the houses in my street and in my block are new but people seem to think it's still the old housing trust homes and the dilapidated old homes that were here before. Perhaps because they haven't been here for a long time. (Homebuyer H7)

I think that there is still the misconception that Mitchell Park was Mitchell Park. Unless you've driven through the area and have seen recent changes, people tend to drive along main roads and still from Mitchell Park, well that used to be lots of housing trust and unless you get in there and have a look you don't see the changes. I still think they think it's still very much a housing trust area, housing commission area. I played sport for Mitchell Park Football Club and the misconception that Mitchell Park is still very much a low socioeconomic suburb is not really valid. (Private renter MP118)

I know a lot of people would say you wouldn't want to go and live there [Mitchell Park] but er, I think it is just wonderful the development that has happened. (Social housing tenant MP2)

I think the people who have known the area for a long time, the people who haven't known of it say well whereabouts is that. Ah that new area with the bricked thing! And I say yeah, yeah that's it. Or if I see them with eyebrows lift up I say it's a new estate then [laughter] I'm not living in a housing trust home. (Homeowner MP98)

I think there's still a bit of stereotyping. That's not going to be broken down until people come and experience it themselves. (Private renter N84)

Stigma, social mix and segregation discourses

At the opposite end of the continuum, other respondents (essentially homeowners) expressed a 'segregation' type of discourse that objected to the mix of housing tenure groups in the neighbourhoods, and to the presence of social housing in particular. First and foremost the presence of social housing in the local neighbourhood was depicted as an enduring cause of neighbourhood stigma. This group advocated separation between the different housing tenure groups. From this perspective, social mix was expressed as undesirable at least in terms of propinquity of different housing tenure groups at the local scale. Tenure segregation was seen to be a better option than the varied social mix that had been implemented. Some of these respondents felt that there should not be any social housing in the neighbourhood:

Why is there no housing trust in Mitcham or Burnside? Why does there have to be a mix of SAHT and homeowners in Mitchell Park? (Homeowner MP1)

Respondents espousing this 'segregation' discourse pointed to pockets of social housing as constituting the stigmatised parts of the neighbourhood. They highlighted specific streets where social housing was still located as problematic parts of the neighbourhood with poor reputations. These locales were sometimes described as 'danger zones' and 'bad places' where it was felt unsafe to walk at night and were commonly referred to as 'the SAHT part of the neighbourhood'. Objections were often expressed about the antisocial behaviours of some social housing tenants.

One day it was like being in New York. I looked out my window, and I could see these cars and police officers in vests with guns, and swarming around the outside of the house. Then there was this big attack, and they grabbed the girl and dragged her, and she bit someone, and they had an ambulance. And it was like the streets of New York here! (Homeowner MP9)

[I] don't like to stereotype or whatever but there are some bad areas, streets I don't like to walk down at night [name of street] being one of them ... I have

> *heard of people, there's a lady riding her bike has had things thrown at her as she rides her bike she works at night as she works as a cleaner up at Flinders [local hospital]. (Homebuyer MP3)*

This segregation discourse about social mix was also linked to lowered feelings of pride about the neighbourhood. A number of the homeowners and private renters expressed the specific view, for instance, that social housing tenants lacked pride in their homes and that a varied tenure mix was a barrier to improving the reputations of the neighbourhoods:

> *'Cause I can tell you going down my street which ones are the housing trust, which ones are the rentals by the rubbish they are leaving out in the street. Dumping it alongside the road, that sort of attitude, and what it actually does is, actually instead of pulling up those who are in the lower socioeconomic group it actually dumbs down, it drags down the neighbourhood. (Homeowner MP7)*

> *There are one or two streets that I wouldn't want to live in. That's mainly probably because they are housing commission homes and you might find that obviously the people that live in those homes are maybe of a poorer quality of life or something like that but that I suppose is being judgemental. It might be a very nice street to live in but I wouldn't live in it. When you look at the home and the way it has been let go, you wouldn't want to live next to somewhere like that I think. (Private renter MP118)*

> *The problem with it [social housing] is that there are still pockets. Like that street opposite me, it is a pocket of housing trust people and you can tell it. (Homeowner MP9)*

An interesting finding was that the increased mix of private rental housing in the neighbourhoods attracted a similar segregation type of discourse. In particular, objections were raised about the high turnover of tenants in private rental. Comments were also made about investors purchasing newer houses for sale to subsequently rent on the private rental market, which was identified as detracting from the residents' sense of pride in the neighbourhoods as the houses were often not well maintained. An interrelated issue was raised about the sales of the older non-refurbished social housing on the private market. While the SAHT upgraded the housing that remained in their hands for public rental and attempted to blend it into the neighbourhood, the surplus housing was often purchased in bulk by private landlords without a commitment to upgrading it. Respondents pointed out that this housing was often very run-down and detracted from the overall attractiveness of the neighbourhood:

Probably we have more trouble with the private rental ones, of the old transportable ones – one down the street here. We've had problems with various people who have been in there. (Social housing tenant H35)

We have one next door [private rental] and they don't look after it, he couldn't care less. (Homeowner N161)

There are a couple of houses I can think of here in the Hillcrest area I wouldn't like to live next door to either because of the type of tenant or the landlord basically not giving a damn about the property. Just simply renting it to whoever without a lot of effort. Just simply to get the rent money and not spend a lot of money on the property. (Homeowner H155)

Stigma consciousness

Many of the social housing tenants that were interviewed seemed acutely aware that there was still some stigma attached to the social housing tenure emanating internally from other residents. A respondent at Mitchell Park, for instance, reported that one of their neighbours (in a cluster of units) did not want other residents within the neighbourhood to know that their units were social housing. From this perspective, the broader tenure mix and related extensive refurbishments that had taken place, along with efforts to blend the renovated and newly built social housing with private housing, were depicted as useful strategies. It had reduced the likelihood of social housing tenants being readily identifiable:

And he said 'ah I'd never tell anyone this is housing trust', I said 'really why?' 'Ah no he said'. But there's nothing, no one would know, you know, they'd just think, ah a nice group of units. All the garden out the front was established by the trust and it's all nice and neat and tidy. We've each done our own things in our backyard and I thought that's really sad ... It's a beautiful unit. How lucky are we, how lucky are we! That's his view that's how he feels about it, so I guess it's not really for me to say one way or another whether it's right or wrong but it's a shame because he's not going to add to the area becoming better though. (Social housing tenant MP2)

Other social housing respondents also articulated this awareness of stigma consciousness:

Some people think that I'm a homeowner and they're in housing trust. Some of them think you're all homeowners. I say 'I'm in a rented house too don't worry about it' some people do get a stigma about having to rent. (Social housing tenant MP266)

> *I think it's good that you not have housing trust people living in one group because then they're segregated and put into one box where everyone's the same like and everybody seems to look down on some people who are in HT [housing trust] like they're just like they're all bums or something, I don't know where they get this idea but that's not so. There are a minority of people who go into trust homes and don't look after them and I think by separating them and splitting them up and putting them in a development area where there's private rental, trust, whatever, is a good idea because then you don't know ... which are housing trust homes and which are not. My house certainly does not look like a HT home. (Social housing tenant H2R)*

> *Because you know, I think you need, like you have the elite, the private homes that you know, some do think they're elite don't they. And then the public housing. You've got to have it. Just because they live in public housing doesn't mean to say that you're not a good person. I know, I think it's a good idea [social mix]. You've got to have that mix. (Social housing tenant MPSC)*

> *It's sort of the image they're portraying. And people read that and are affected by it. And that's exactly what I was saying to [child's name] this morning that you are affected by what you read and so on and so on. And if you see this image constantly of negativity then you think that's all that goes on around you. (Social housing tenant MP192)*

In articulating these views, these social housing tenants illustrated the adoption of similar coping strategies to those identified by Reutter *et al.* (2009: 300) in their study of residents of low-income neighbourhoods in Canada. Respondents in Reutter's study talked about 'being labelled' and 'looked at and treated differently'. The study found that participants living in poverty have a profound awareness of stigma and a sense that in some ways they are culpable for their predicament. Their coping strategies include concealing their discreditable status and managing the sense of dislocation between how they think they are perceived (virtual) and how they feel (actual). This may also help to explain the unexpected finding in another study that for social housing tenants the quality of housing after urban renewal had a greater impact on their residential satisfaction than place amenities or social networks (Baker and Arthurson 2007). It may be that the newer or upgraded housing that is less identifiable as social housing ameliorates primary level stigma consciousness. The mechanism at work is merely by virtue of concealing the discreditable status of social housing tenants from the eyes of their neighbours. The nub of the issue is that the housing acts as an impediment to stigma as the social housing tenants are no longer easily identified.

Another interesting finding in the current study was that many of the social housing tenants who had become homeowners, often through purchase opportunities provided by the urban renewal project, were then keen to differentiate themselves from the social housing tenure. This viewpoint was expressed through employing a segregation type of discourse that associated concentrations of social housing with increased stigma, even though the homeowners drawing on these depictions had until recently themselves lived in the social housing tenure:

> *A lot of them are trouble. It puts your [house] value down, I think, if you've got them [social housing tenants] all around. A lot of people don't notice who they are, but I do. (Homeowner, previous social housing tenant H55)*

> *I think there's a better class of person coming into the place because of this [redevelopment] ... Although we will always have a certain amount because the housing trust have built units you know in different parts for different people in the area. (Homeowner, previous social housing tenant N282)*

Once again this is similar to the findings of Reutter *et al.* (2009: 300), in which, in some instances, the strategies adopted by low-income residents to cope with stigma included engaging in a form of cognitive dissonance. In the current study, this point is highlighted by a segregation discourse that was adopted by recent homeowners that had moved out of social housing. They were then keen to distance themselves from social housing tenants in the same or similar circumstances. This situation also emerged in earlier research conducted in the Hillcrest urban renewal area that explored residents' acceptance of socioeconomic diversity and the new mix of social and private housing (Biggins and Hassan 1998: 39). The highest approval for the new socioeconomically mixed community came from low-income earners (79.4%) and residents on high incomes (65%), while middle-income respondents approved the least (40%). It seems there is greater disapproval of a mixed-income community where social distance is smaller, that is, residents want to distance themselves from those in the income strata below them.

Conclusions

This chapter explored residents' perspectives about the links between neighbourhood reputation, stigma and social mix. The findings overall suggested, at least from the viewpoint of residents across the different housing tenure groups, that changing the social mix through introducing homeowners onto the social housing estates as part of renewal initiatives had improved the overall reputation of the neighbourhoods. Two dominant types of discourse were identified. One group of respondents expressed an integration discourse that supported the benefits of a broad social mix within the neighbourhood. They described the heterogeneous social mix incorporating the diversity of the different housing tenures in positive terms depicting it as an important way for social housing tenants to blend into the neighbourhood and avoid the stigma attached to their housing tenure. They often recognised that stigma is about structural inequality rather than the concentration of social housing. Another group of respondents (predominantly homeowners) espoused a segregation discourse that saw social mix as problematic. They identified the mere presence of social housing in the neighbourhood as burdensome and as attracting stigma to the area. These homeowners tended to associate social housing tenants with problems of antisocial behaviour within their neighbourhoods often drawing on a segregation discourse that was akin to the 'pathological' discourse identified in Hastings' (2004) study. Like the pathological discourse that Hastings identified, an account of poverty and disadvantage was provided that focussed on the unacceptable behaviours of some individuals. However, in the current situation, the segregation discourse was associated with specific clusters of social housing in particular streets and generated from some social housing. In effect, though, all social housing tenants were tarred with the same brush. This is not surprising given that individuals entering social housing are increasingly high need and complex tenants. In view of this situation, the stigma attached to social housing is likely to increase rather than dissipate. The key point of difference was that Hastings found these viewpoints expressed predominantly from people who were not familiar with the neighbourhoods rather than from within the neighbourhoods, as in the current study. Within the segregation discourse contradictory notions were espoused. On the one hand the concentration of social housing was identified as a problem and deconcentration was seen as important. On the other hand, homeowners in this group of respondents did not want to reside next door to or even near social housing tenants. They expressed the view that it would be better not to have any social housing in the neighbourhood.

An interesting finding was that, in some instances, the segregation discourse was also linked to the increased mix of private rental housing in the neighbourhoods. Respondents noted that often the houses were not well maintained, as the function was merely to obtain rental income for absentee landlords. The findings suggest that from the viewpoint of many of the residents interviewed, the private rental tenure is increasingly becoming associated with stigma in regenerated neighbourhoods. This finding raises questions, as the balance of housing assistance in Australia is moving to favour provision of subsidies for private rental assistance, and affordable rental housing funded through private landlords as opposed to social housing supplied through government.

The nuanced accounts that emerged in the interviews about the day-to-day life in the three case study neighbourhoods suggested that social housing tenants internalised some of the stigma attached to the tenure by some of their homeowner neighbours. They felt unfairly discriminated against and expressed a profound sense of stigma consciousness and at the same time resented being perceived as different. While they often expressed support for social mix, the impact of housing design was the key factor acknowledged that helped them fit into the neighbourhood through making them unidentifiable as social housing tenants.

Overall, residents' discourses about social mix were different to those adopted by policymakers. In particular, the discourses that were evident showed no awareness of policy discourses about social inclusion and social exclusion. Then again, like policymakers, residents used tenure mix as a proxy for socioeconomic mix. They viewed them as similar terms with similar meanings and used them interchangeably.

References

Arthurson K (2001) Achieving social justice in estate regeneration: the impact of physical image construction. *Housing Studies* **16**, 807–826.

Arthurson K (2004) From stigma to demolition: Australian debates about housing and social exclusion. *Journal of Housing and the Built Environment* **19**, 255–270.

Baker E and Arthurson K (2007) Housing, place or social networks: what's more important for relocating tenants? *Australian Planner* **44**(4), 28–35.

Biggins N and Hassan PR (1998) 'Northfield precinct one, a review of the social objectives'. Department of Sociology, Flinders University of South Australia, Adelaide.

Darcy M (2009) De-concentration of disadvantage and mixed income housing: a critical discourse approach. *Housing, Theory and Society* **27**, 1–22.

Hastings A (2004) Stigma and social housing estates: beyond pathological explanations. *Journal of Housing and the Built Environment* **19**, 233–254, doi: 10.1007/s10901-004-0723-y.

Link B and Phelan J (2001) Conceptualising stigma. *Annual Review of Sociology* **27**, 363–385.

Musterd S (2008) Residents' views on social mix: social mix, social networks and stigmatisation in post-war housing estates in Europe. *Urban Studies* **45**, 897–915.

Peel M (2003) *Lowest Rung: Voices of Australian Poverty*. Cambridge University Press, New York.

Permentier M, Van Ham M and Bolt G (2009) Neighbourhood reputation and the intention to leave the neighbourhood. *Environment and Planning* **A41**, 2162–2180.

Reutter L, Veenstra G, Love R and Raphael DME (2009) Who do they think they are, anyway? Perceptions of and responses to poverty stigma. *Qualitative Health Research* **19**, 297–311.

8

Sense of community, social cohesion and social mix

Introduction

> *[Governments] cannot make people like, talk with, or help their neighbours.*
> *(Johnston 2003: 17)*

This seems a pertinent statement to start the chapter with as the opposite rationale underlies current support for instigating social mix policies in neighbourhoods of concentrated social housing. In implementing contemporary neighbourhood renewal projects, policymakers and planners argue that for impoverished residents there are numerous benefits in thinning out spatial concentrations of social housing and developing mixed-income communities. A persistent idea throughout the history of social mix, up to and including the present day, is that spatial propinquity of middle-income residents and less advantaged neighbours will provide aspirational role models. Beyond the expectations of role modelling, greater heterogeneity of residents across different housing tenures and income levels is linked to an increased sense of community and social cohesion than where homogeneity of social housing dominates. However, as detailed in preceding chapters, research findings and academic debates suggest that strongly cohesive communities already exist on some homogeneous social housing estates, invalidating the notion that a balanced social mix is necessary for building inclusive communities (Arthurson 2002; Tesoriero 2003). In addition, placing residents with different lifestyles in close proximity in a neighbourhood may result in conflict, so such policies need to be pursued carefully (Beekman *et al.* 2001). The tacit enquiry that is left unsaid is whether it is possible for housing authorities to create their envisaged 'inclusive' and 'cohesive' communities by changing social mix at a neighbourhood level. As Atkinson and Kintrea (2000) have argued in the UK regeneration context, it is one thing to suggest that social networks and who people mix with are important, but quite another to propose that through introducing middle-income homeowners into social housing estates, governments can rebuild more socially integrated, cohesive and inclusive communities. Furthermore, some important implications of changing social mix on existing communities have been given little consideration in current debates and the voices of residents have rarely been heard. This chapter further examines the in-depth interviews with residents and presents their perspectives on the links between social mix and the sense of community and social cohesion within the three case study neighbourhoods.

Interview findings

In engaging respondents in discussions about their perspectives of the sense of community and social cohesion in their neighbourhood, and whether they thought these aspects were related to social mix, four major themes emerged: the sense of closeness between residents in the neighbourhood; friendliness and friendships; whether residents share the same or different values, tolerance of differences and how people get along with each other; and trust and willingness to assist neighbours.

Sense of community and closeness within the neighbourhood

When respondents talked about the sense of community and feelings of closeness between people in the neighbourhood, as in the explorations of stigma, an integration type of discourse about social mix was evident. It was suggested that day-to-day life was mainly pleasant and that there was a sense that a community existed in the newly mixed-tenure neighbourhoods. This group of respondents sometimes described their neighbourhood as:

> *Quiet, peaceful, no issue with neighbours, convenient to shops, close to city ... I'm really happy here. (Private renter H108)*

As highlighted above, respondents often related the improved amenity of the physical environment and availability of local services and infrastructure, such as parks and reserves, with an enhanced sense of community in the neighbourhood.

I don't have a problem with the neighbourhood; I think it's good. The neighbourhood's good. The facilities around there are great. I love the community. (Social housing tenant N70)

However, the provision of improved facilities was in no way linked with arguments about social mix espoused by policymakers in the 1960s and 1970s. Then, the presence of middle-income homeowners was supported as leading to an increased revenue base for the local council and funding for crucial infrastructure to improve the neighbourhood and equity between the classes.

Once again, as in discussions about neighbourhood reputation and stigma, some respondents expressed a segregation discourse that raised objections about the increased mix of private renters in the neighbourhoods. The throughput of private renters that moved frequently into and out of the neighbourhoods was described as making it difficult to develop a sense of community. From this particular perspective the private rental tenure was linked to a lack of community or social integration. One respondent summarised the common objections stating that the private rental house directly opposite their home was occupied by three different groups of people over the preceding two-year period.

I see that the private rental people are not going to stay for very long. Like six months. (Homebuyer H7)

This situation was clearly expressed as detracting from opportunities to develop a more stable and close-knit community that was composed of longer-term residents that had a commitment to staying in the neighbourhood and working to enhance the sense of community.

For other respondents there was no notion of any sense of community existing at all or of the local neighbourhood being close-knit. Instead, feelings of social isolation were sometimes articulated:

Well I feel very lonely here, which is really awful. (Social housing tenant MP192)

A segregation discourse was again unequivocally expressed by some homeowners that disapproved of the social mix, particularly the presence of social housing in the neighbourhood. Social housing was depicted as working against the development of a sense of community or social cohesion.

I'm a little bit disappointed with the council and government who wanted to integrate [social] housing tenants amongst other normal, average down the road people. Well the idea might have sounded good but I don't think it's worked ... It makes it neighbourhood mediocrity. That's what you come out with that's the outcome because the people who are quiet and want to get on with their neighbours they become submissive to these people the way they behave. They're frightened of them. They might put a rock like my neighbour who had a car tyre coming down the road into her bedroom. (Homeowner MP1)

Before there were all mainly the same types of people and now there are huge differences. Like your really poor and really wealthy. Not wealthy but much better off people and I think they don't mix. (Homeowner H7)

From this perspective, there was no expectation that social mix would contribute to middle class role modelling, rather it was seen as an imposition that led to problems of antisocial behaviour in neighbourhoods, which worked against community cohesion.

A different discourse was adopted by other residents across the three housing tenure groups, often the retired or elderly residents, that was distinct from both the segregation and integration discourses previously identified. These respondents were categorised as 'neutralisers', as they either pointed out that revised 'social mix' meant that less mixing was likely to occur between residents, or they perceived social mix as irrelevant to the sense of community or closeness of residents in the neighbourhood. Neutralisers stated, for instance, that many of the new homeowners that had bought into the regenerated neighbourhoods were working hard to pay their mortgages and consequently tended not to spend much time in the neighbourhoods or frequent local shops. Respondents argued that this situation was not conducive to the development of closeness between residents or a sense of community. These findings question how many people in contemporary society who are busy working and bringing up families have the time or inclination to be involved in extensive community activities or mixing with their neighbours. In turn, why do we place these expectations on residents of lower income neighbourhoods but ignore the self-imposed segregation of wealthier people who choose to live among similar socioeconomic groups in gated neighbourhoods? In part, the issue may stem from the origins of social mix policies, which were based on (now outdated) ideals of families with one breadwinner at work and women at home caring for children. For most modern-day middle-income homeowners this is far from reality, as over the past decade house prices have appreciated substantially, requiring two incomes to service large home loans (Gabriel *et al.* 2005). Respondents described the realities of their circumstances:

You never see anybody. These girls over here, there's two I think. As far as I know you see the two come together, they are nurses and they are on shift work, so you never see them. And I think the other side, the lady, she's new too, and I never see her. (Social housing tenant MP270)

I go to work every day early in the morning, I come home at night and I don't connect with my neighbours. So their whole theory around social mix is that it is meant to help people, but that is not necessarily happening in society today. (Private renter N204)

The main thing about the whole area and I think it applies to most, is that neighbours don't talk so much. Not all of them ... It's part of the reason I think that people don't talk because their mothers are not here in the daytime to pick up the kids. They don't mingle. (Homeowner N6)

Studies have also found that social housing tenants have lower levels of motor vehicle ownership than other housing tenure groups and for this reason are more likely to spend their time locally, using local shops and services. In contrast, middle-income residents more frequently go out of the neighbourhood to work and shop and to participate in leisure activities (Atkinson and Kintrea 2000). For the latter group, the generalised access to motor vehicles and new technologies means that the local neighbourhood or community is less relevant, as they conduct their working and social life at lengthy distances from where they live, which results in less interaction with other residents (Cass *et al.* 2005). The results suggest that the different housing tenure groups lead parallel lives and may not often cross paths.

Friendliness and friendships

A similar theme about the demands of the modern lifestyle making social mix less relevant for day-to-day life emerged when respondents talked about the friendliness of their neighbourhood. Once again, the 'neutraliser' discourse was dominant, as residents basically perceived social mix as irrelevant to the friendliness of the neighbourhood and whether or not friendships developed between residents. In general, respondents expressed the viewpoint that they were too busy to mix with their neighbours and whether they were in the same or a different housing tenure was of little importance. Typical responses were that:

Over the time we've been here, it's become less friendly. But that seems to be the way of most neighbourhoods now, because neighbours just don't talk to each other. They're too busy, they have insufficient time or they're not interested ... and I think both parties are working and they don't get a lot of time. (Homeowner N6)

Not particularly [friendly]. The people in the units well on the other side of the driveway are really nice people and the one back here is nice but I don't see much of them, we're not in each other's pockets, which is a good thing. (Social housing tenant MP192)

The older residents that are in the older style homes but are still homeowners are friendly. The houses are older, but they've been here like forever so they're nice ... many months ago I wasn't aware of so many things because my baby was small and I didn't go out as much. But now I'm out and about a lot more like daily I see a lot of things that I didn't see before and that is it's not as friendly as I thought it was. (Homebuyer H7)

Some of the social housing tenants that were relocated from adjacent or nearby neighbourhoods as part of the renewal projects mentioned that they often maintained coexisting links and ties with their old neighbourhoods:

We do keep in touch with the neighbours from the other one [old neighbourhood]. We pop down every now and then and say hello and how are you. We do, yes. They're elderly neighbours and they loved to see the kids. The kids would drop in, take their bikes for a ride and ... yeah, they've grown up with them ... seen them born. (Social housing tenant N70)

This finding is by no means novel and supports the results of international studies in which some social housing residents relocated to new mixed-tenure neighbourhoods still had links and social ties with their old neighbourhoods (see, for instance, Briggs 1998).

In contrast, other respondents felt that the different tenures 'mix in pretty well' drawing on an integration discourse about social mix:

The majority of people are friendly and nice; you know I've always had good people around me. (Social housing tenant H2R)

Next door she's on her own. We don't go to each other's place or anything like that. We just talk over the fence and change VCRs and all that sort of thing but we don't live in each other's place. I've never done that. (Social housing tenant MP270)

Well we've all moved in at the same time so we've all bonded right from the first moment more or less. And I think that's the beauty of new neighbourhoods like this, you know because everybody's new and I noticed just moving around and seeing people out and about that we have obviously got a really good, what's the word? Multicultural mix of families and we go past and they're out with the little children playing football or something out the front and it's just nice ... they'll always nod or smile say hello and that's good you know I think that's really good. Because where we'd been living before you'd be lucky half the time for anybody to acknowledge you or even be there. I think it's just lovely; it's really friendly and nice. My husband feels the same way too, we feel so settled and happy here. (Social housing tenant MP2)

It was also suggested that residents did not really have a choice about not accepting the revised tenure mix in the neighbourhood because:

> *A lot of people poke their nose up ... they can't do anything about it, you've got to live there. (Homeowner N282)*

As Jupp (1999) argued, interaction is likely to be too minor to make any difference to social integration and the related anticipated benefits of social mix. This viewpoint is reflected in the following remarks made by respondents:

> *I see a few of these people [social housing tenants] as I walk to work. I say 'gidday, how are you going?' because I've lived here for so long. I don't mix with them socially but I do have a chat, say 'your garden looks nice' and you know to be pleasant. We probably don't mix socially. Even your absolute next-door neighbour, you don't always catch up with them. (Homeowner MP45)*

> *And I would say that it's friendly but not close, so people smile at each other in the street but they don't necessarily know each other well. In our little set of units here, it has taken us two and a half years to get to know our neighbours ... and we know our neighbour across the driveway very well because he is not very nice. (Private renter N204)*

The mix of children within the community

For some respondents, social mix was clearly interpreted as the age mix of residents within the neighbourhood. In particular, the mix of children and elderly residents was identified as important in relation to the friendliness of residents and the potential for cultivating friendships. Respondents verbalised an integration discourse that identified the presence of children as particularly amenable to developing friendships across different socioeconomic groups, an argument that is also consistent within the international literature. However, once again the level of interaction described was often perfunctory, involving activities such as waving or saying hello in the street rather than developing firm friendships:

> *One person on one side keeps very much to himself. He'll wave and that's probably it. The people on the other side, our two youngest kids play with them. You might get an acknowledgement occasionally from them ... think that's the trend now, anyway. People tend not to be quite as friendly. (Social housing tenant N70)*

This integration discourse specifically linked the presence of children at local schools as facilitating higher levels of mixing between residents across the different housing tenure groups:

When the girls were at the primary school, and that's just down the road, there'd be lots of single mothers bringing their kids to school who lived a matter of streets away. And myself, we own our home, you've got a lot of single parents, and we all talk and get on well together. (Homeowner H98)

Being in the school, we have all the mixture of the Hillcrest community in there. You've got all walks of community. You've just got to go in the car park in the morning and its mind-boggling the cars you see there. There will be a sports car or there will be a beautiful four-wheel-drive and you think, my God, it's just amazing that all these different people live in this area and they all go to this one public school and they play together as one, or try to. (Social housing tenant H2R)

I think people tend to mix with all of the neighbours if your kids are perhaps going to kindergarten or school. That's where we got to know more people. (Homeowner MP45)

This is consistent with other contemporary research findings (Jupp 1999; Atkinson and Kintrea 2000; Allen *et al.* 2005; Holmes 2006). However, another study found little evidence of social interaction between different housing tenure groups despite children attending the same schools (Beekman *et al.* 2001). A mitigating factor is that middle-income residents often purposely decide to send their children to schools outside the local neighbourhood, especially when the quality of local schools is perceived as less than optimal, as highlighted by Stenson and Watt (1999) in the UK.

There were also instances of this in the current study, as articulated by this homeowner:

And unfortunately with that type of housing [social housing] I think still comes those sort of people I guess. The low income. My children don't go to the local school because of that. It was a violent school. (Homeowner N49)

The age mix of residents is also important

Respondents commonly talked about social mix in relation to the age of residents in the neighbourhood as well as the mix of incomes and housing tenures. They pointed out that, with estate renewal, not only were more homeowners moving into the neighbourhoods but there was a broader age mix of residents. They expressed the view that intergenerational diversity impacted on opportunities to develop friendships. While many of the elderly were longer-term residents and welcoming to others in the neighbourhood, it was pointed out that the different age groups often lead divergent lifestyles, which might preclude them from coming into contact with each other. This factor has received little attention in the literature on social mix or in the policy discourses. As the following respondent explains, younger people, for instance, are often working hard to pay the mortgage or are out socialising and do not spend a lot of time in the neighbourhood. In contrast, frail or disabled elderly people are more likely to spend their time in the neighbourhood or perhaps become housebound.

> *Some of them [neighbours] are young, some are middle-aged, some older. There's quite a mixture that are buying here. There were some young people living up the road on the right hand side, but you don't really see much of them, because they're young and they're working hard ... And then you've got elderly people living in these houses that don't get out much of the time. (Social housing tenant H2R)*

Others expanded on this theme, arguing that within contemporary society parents are more fearful and protective of children than they were in the past:

> *The neighbourhood is not friendly ... because of the social mix. You've either got the really elderly people who are friendly, or you've got your cautious young couples with kids. Because of the really awful things happening with paedophiles and stuff like that, I think people are really sheltered and they hold on to kids and don't let them out of their sight. So it's not so friendly with the young. (Homeowner H7)*

Overall, the findings imply that many homebuyers work long hours to service mortgages and generally lead busy lives that are not wholly tied to the local neighbourhood, which means that there is often little time or inclination for mixing with other residents, no matter what housing tenure they reside in. However, in the current study, as in the international literature, a discourse emerged that saw children attending local schools as a factor that facilitated social interaction across different housing tenure groups.

Sharing the same values, tolerance of differences and getting along with each other

Some of the biggest tensions that arose in interviews were around what were often perceived as insurmountable differences between residents' values and standards of behaviour. In particular, the 'older' and established social housing tenants, who were often elderly and had lived in social housing a long time, expressed a segregation type of discourse about the social mix of the newer, more complex and high need tenants currently entering the social housing tenure. Several of these more established and long-term social housing tenants depicted some of the difficult situations they regularly encountered with the newer tenants, often their immediate neighbours:

> *Oh, the language, they used to swear like anything and it was terrible, you could hear them all, the kiddies ... She couldn't care less but they were terrible children. Amazing how they get these homes, people like that ... Oh, it was funny, it was like Coronation Street! I'm glad there're gone, anyhow. (Social housing tenant MP6)*

> *She's bipolar and her and her kids fight all the time and they yell and scream and slam doors, so I rang the housing trust, probably three months ago. She started at three o'clock in the morning and she went right through ... and I just couldn't take any more so I waited and got the housing trust and I complained. They rang her and told her that it was unacceptable. She was quiet for three weeks and they rang me back and asked me. I said that so far she'd been quiet, but it's not going to last. (Social housing tenant N56)*

> *The housing trust built them a brand new house and put them in with shutters and they have just destroyed it and they go to school and they destroy things there. I banned the girl from the canteen for a year. She was rude and she stole from the lunch crate, money ... Those sort of people annoy me. Because they have been given a brand new beautiful house in a beautiful area and they have destroyed that whole area. Ruined it! Two people have sold their house and moved because of them. The woman that lives at the back of them works at the post office. She's had a gutful, she's called even the local MP, she's done everything, people are selling up. They're just foul-mouthed disgusting animals is what they're called by every neighbour that lives around them. (Social housing tenant H2R)*

Importantly, what this situation illustrates is that social housing tenants are not one homogeneous mass or 'underclass' as is often depicted by the rationales underlying social mix policies. There was clearly social distancing within the social housing tenure from respondents such as these. They expressed a segregation discourse about the social mix within social housing and its relationship to social cohesion based on their perceptions of what constitutes 'good' and 'bad' social housing tenants.

In comparison, particularly from some homeowners, no such distinction was made about the social mix within social housing. There was little tolerance expressed of social housing tenants *per se*, together depicted as an undifferentiated and problematic tenure group. This uniform image was reflected through a segregation discourse that portrayed social housing tenants as very different from themselves, with undesirable and typically opposing values:

> *We knew about that, we knew it had a housing trust, unfortunately a lower quality of life if you like to put it that way, and 'cause over the last 10 years that's*

changed quite a bit. A lot of older people have moved into the area on the courtyard blocks. So obviously a lot of new houses are here but it will probably be another 20 years before there is a real change. (Homeowner MP1)

I think the poorer people think that the richer people are snobs and the richer people think that you're not good enough to say hello to perhaps. I don't know. But I see that there's a bit of snobbery going on. I don't think that the groups interact well. Not at all that's what I think. I don't think the low-income tenants [social housing] mind that there are nicer newer homes being built around the corner but I think that the high income earners wish that the housing trust units and stuff would get knocked down quicker and that more homeowners would be placed here. And they know that will happen. And this is not being prejudiced either. Trying not to be prejudiced. Sometimes I think that the low-income earners are kind of not happy to be poorer. But it doesn't look like they're trying to do anything to improve their situation. They don't seem to try and better themselves. (Homebuyer H7)

Other social housing respondents and homeowners expressed an integration discourse that encompassed some of the older arguments about social mix. They depicted spatial propinquity of different housing tenure groups as beneficial for everyone. This was not in the sense of providing role models of appropriate behaviours but rather in terms of denoting a way to build awareness of the commonalities between them and to build up tolerance of alternative ways of life. The arguments were presented in much the same way that the debates about cross-class fertilisation of ideas and habits were constructed in the redistributive policy debates of the 1950s and 1960s, which saw heterogeneity as a means to benefit rich and poor residents alike.

It's beneficial for the kids, for everybody growing up in the area, its more social, you meet different people in life, you get to learn respect and to value other people's opinions and property. It is a different setup and I think it's working for the best. I think they should have done it a long time ago. (Social housing tenant H2R)

The timber house I had was an eyesore when I took it over. And within six months I had everyone in that street coming up and congratulating me for doing it up, putting a garden in and making it look real nice as if this house and this property had looked like a dump for years. So it is what you make of it. And I think people around you if they see that you're looking after your property and you know, you're not throwing wild parties or anything, they respect you no matter what. No matter whether you're a housing trust tenant or not and 'cause I certainly don't like living next to someone that has got cars all in the front yard and crap around the backyard and it's stinking. I think it's disgusting. (Social housing tenant H2R)

People need variety to start with. Where you have got areas with all public housing tenants you have got everybody on a low income, which is why they are in public housing for whatever reason and it's really easy to be demoralised by that. (Social housing tenant MP192)

For some reason or other housing trust people don't seem to have a good name and yet the people that I know here were very nice people. They were from Scotland and they were very nice people. I know someone else over in Mansfield Park ... she's a really lovely lady ... I've known her for 35 years and she's still living in that same house 35 years later. Through no fault of her own why she's in a housing trust home. She chose to leave her husband and not take anything so she had nothing. That's how she ended up being in housing trust. She's got a good education and she always keeps her house nice and tidy. (Homebuyer H40)

Trust and willingness to help neighbours

Another theme that was evident in the interviews surrounded trust and willingness to help neighbours. Some respondents mentioned that, although they do not have a lot to do with their neighbours:

I know that if I need help they are available. (Private renter H108)

Other respondents provided instances of how neighbours had provided unsolicited but nonetheless welcomed support:

We have a delightful elderly couple living across from us ... they're just lovely and they actually were relocated from Mansfield Park ... So now they are closer to family and you know we've had them over for a meal and we've been over there for a meal and oh they are gorgeous, they're really delightful. And you know if they haven't seen us around for a while he comes knocking on the door, you know just seeing if you're okay. (Social housing tenant MP2)

The old lady across the road doesn't speak English but brings over cakes. (Homeowner MP7)

Oh, I keep to myself a lot. The only person I really talk to is the guy across the road, and another that used to live across in that wood and iron place. Just after I moved here, he sold that in the November. I moved here in the May. But he

> *calls around to see how I'm going. And if ever I want anything done, the guy across will come over and do it for me, like pictures hung or things like that. He hung all these because I haven't got a straight eye. (Social housing tenant N56)*

Conclusions

In the interviews, residents evoked two dominant discourses about social mix and the sense of community and social cohesion in their neighbourhood. These were similar to the integration and segregation discourses that were identified when exploring the issues of neighbourhood stigma and reputation. Residents utilising the integration discourse were positive about the neighbourhood social mix and identified that the different housing tenure groups got along well with each other. However, this situation was moderated by the low levels of contact that occurred, which seemed unlikely to lead to the increased social cohesion or role modelling envisioned by contemporary policymakers. Nevertheless, for some of the social housing respondents and homeowners, the integration discourse encompassed historical arguments about social mix. They depicted spatial propinquity of different housing tenure groups as beneficial for everyone. These arguments were never presented in the sense of providing role models of appropriate behaviours but rather in terms of expanding awareness and understanding of the connections between different socioeconomic groups and building tolerance of dissimilar circumstances and lifestyles. The arguments were similar to the ideas of cross-class fertilisation of ideas and habits from the 1950s and 1960s, which perceived heterogeneity of housing tenures as a benefit to wealthier and poorer residents alike.

Conversely, a segregation type of discourse was espoused mostly from homeowners that resented the social mix in their neighbourhood, particularly the presence of social housing, which was depicted as working against a sense of community or social cohesion. Social housing tenants were represented in a uniform image as one homogeneous group that was responsible for antisocial behaviour in the neighbourhoods. These depictions were at odds with social housing tenants' understandings that there are 'good' and 'bad' social housing tenants. The bad tenants were predominantly identified as those increasingly entering social housing, and currently listed as high priority by policymakers. Good tenants were the elderly that had resided in social housing for a long time.

In addition to segregation and integration, another discourse was articulated, categorised here as neutralisers. This category of respondents from across the different housing tenure groups expressed two basic arguments that were distinct from both the segregation and integration discourses. Respondents were either agnostic about social mix or simply perceived it as an irrelevant feature of the neighbourhood in relation to the sense of community or closeness of residents.

Busy lifestyle was highlighted as an important aspect of modern life that detracted from the development of community and meant that many residents no longer knew their neighbours or had time to socialise. Many of the new homeowners that had bought into the regenerated neighbourhoods were working hard to pay their mortgages and consequently tended not to spend much time in their neighbourhood. Respondents argued that this situation was not conducive to the development of closeness between residents or a sense of community.

An interesting finding was that residents often talked about social mix in terms of the age of neighbourhood residents. Specifically, they expressed the view that the presence of children was conducive to enhancing the sense of community and friendliness through schools. The elderly and longer-term residents were also identified as more stable groups that generated a sense of community and neighbourliness. These aspects of social mix have received only limited attention in the wider debates about social mix.

The current exploration highlights some of the outdated ideals on which social policies are based. The first of these pertains to the original application of social mix in Australian housing policies to low-income working families, which uniformly consisted of one wage earner and a partner based at home caring for children. Neighbourhoods composed mostly of these types of households are largely redundant, and in the neighbourhoods studied were replaced instead by families experiencing intergenerational unemployment and individuals with high needs juxtaposed with two-income, home owning families. Second, the target groups now entering social housing are mostly people on government pensions, single parent families often with complex social and behavioural issues including ex-prisoners, drug addicts and people with mental health issues being rehabilitated in the community. Both these situations question the relevance of the original ideals of social mix, in which middle class role models would inspire social housing tenants to become homeowners. Home ownership is unlikely to become a reality for the groups currently entering social housing. Third, mobile phones, the internet and social networking technology, and greater access to motor vehicles mean that, for many residents, life is no longer bound to the specific geographical space of the neighbourhood in the way that it was in the past. These circumstances question the original ideals about spatial propinquity facilitating role modelling through social contact between the different classes.

References

Allen M, Camina M, Casey R, Coward S and Wood M (2005) *Mixed Tenure, Twenty Years On – Nothing Out of the Ordinary.* Joseph Rowntree Foundation, York.

Arthurson K (2002) Creating inclusive communities through balancing social mix: a critical relationship or tenuous link? *Urban Policy and Research* **20**, 245–261.

Atkinson A and Kintrea K (2000) Owner occupation, social mix and neighbourhood impacts. *Policy & Politics* **28**, 93–108.

Beekman T, Lyons F and Scott J (2001) 'Improving the understanding of the influence of owner occupiers in mixed-tenure neighbourhoods'. ODS Ltd for Scottish Homes, Edinburgh.

Briggs XD (1998) Brown kids in white suburbs: housing mobility and the many faces of social capital. *Housing Policy Debate* **9**, 177–221.

Cass N, Shove E and Urry J (2005) Social exclusion, mobility and access. *The Sociological Review* **53**, 539–555, doi: 10.1111/j.1467-954X.2005.00565.x.

Gabriel M, Jacobs K, Arthurson K, Burke T and Yates J (2005) 'Conceptualising and measuring the housing affordability problem: national research venture 3: housing affordability for lower income Australians: research paper'. Swinburne University of Technology, Faculty of Life and Social Sciences, Institute for Social Research Australia.

Holmes C (2006) *Mixed Communities, Success and Sustainability.* Joseph Rowntree Foundation, York.

Johnston C (2003) 'Tenancies, communities, and the (re)development of public housing estates – a background paper'. Shelter New South Wales, Sydney.

Jupp B (1999) *Living Together: Community Life on Mixed Housing Estates.* Demos, London.

Stenson K and Watt P (1999) Crime, risk and governance in a southern English village. In *Crime and Conflict in the Countryside.* (Eds G Dingwall and S Moody) pp. 76–93. University of Wales Press, Cardiff.

Tesoriero F (2003) Housing renewal in The Parks community, South Australia. In *Community Practices in Australia.* (Eds W Weeks, J Dixon and L Hoatson) pp. 74–79. Pearson Education, Frenchs Forest, NSW.

9

Conclusions

In concluding, I return to the original questions and key gaps identified in the understandings of social mix policies that directed the pursuit of this book. The first of these concerns was to explore the specific Australian experience with social mix policies. While the US evidence base and literature on neighbourhood effects is often drawn on to support implementation of social mix policies, in the Australian milieu the social mix policies adopted reflect different explanations and social and political contexts for how poverty arises and is best addressed. In the US, the focus is largely on moving people from neighbourhoods with concentrations of disadvantaged people to areas of less poverty and with greater numbers of middle-income neighbours to address issues of race-based spatial segregation. Conversely, Australian efforts largely involve attracting homeowners to areas of concentrated social housing along with relocating social housing tenants to other neighbourhoods to balance the mix of different housing tenures. As explored in the first few chapters of this book, the origins of Australian social mix policies more closely resemble ideas imported from Britain.

In this book unravelling the Australian experience of social mix, the dominant debates by various interest groups were first explored over time, the unexpected consequences of the policies were scrutinised and the perspectives of residents were investigated. Overlaying this enquiry was the wider question of why support for social mix policies re-emerges at particular times, and how we should interpret, for instance, the recently revived enthusiasm for social mix policies in late 20th century and early 21st century Australia.

Social mix as a response to concerns about social class segregation

The historical exploration contained herein identified that the common factor compelling the reinvigoration of ideas about social mix was a response to increasing social segregation between the classes due to large-scale processes of social and industrial change. As awareness and often fear about the consequences of social segregation and spatial concentration of the poor have increased, social mix policies have been advocated as a solution.

In mid-19th century Britain, the idea of social mix was evoked in response to the spatial segregation that developed between the classes due to the growth of new technologies and rapid industrialisation. The invention of factory machinery rendered many workers redundant, and as destitute families flocked to the industrial towns in search of work the towns became overcrowded and unsanitary. As the upper and middle classes began to vacate the towns, undesirable social and sanitary conditions were commonly associated with increasing concentrations of the working classes. The concerns voiced at this time were about social class segregation and the divisions between rich and poor and reflected fears about the poor and the propensity for social unrest that their concentrations and social solidarity afforded. The proposed solutions utilising the notion of social mix became linked to the provision of housing and the planning of industrial towns and cities.

In Britain, the period after the Second World War provided a fecund environment for ideas about social mix to re-emerge. At this stage, social mix was perceived as a mechanism to prevent segregation from increasing between the classes and to try and maintain the perceived level of cooperation and bonding that had occurred during the war effort. This was also an epoch of extensive governmental reforms with the construction of the welfare state and debates about universal service provision. Thus, the concept of social mix was linked to nation-building endeavours and, in particular, the development of new towns between 1945 to the early 1950s. British ideas and perspectives about social mix permeated Australian planning circles in the late 1950s.

Initially, interest in social mix in Australia also reflected concerns about social class segregation. These concerns arose as a response to criticisms about the homogeneity of public housing estates compared with other neighbourhoods in terms of low-income, working tenants that the tenure catered for and the lack of crucial services, such as public transport, shops and health and community services. The idea of a balanced mix of housing tenures and socioeconomic characteristics at the neighbourhood level was embraced as a planning solution to stop recreating these sorts of problems. The social democratic foundations of the SAHT highlighted some of the early redistributive ideals about social mix and the benefits thought to accrue to residents. During the 1970s, support for social mix policies flourished, particularly in South Australian planning circles, where the downturn in manufacturing industry and tightening of public housing eligibility criteria had begun to intensify concentrations of unemployed residents on housing estates.

In the contemporary context, the reinvigoration of support for social mix policies may be similarly linked to new forms of spatial segregation on social housing estates. The segregation illustrates the devastating consequences of a series of social and economic changes and the results of earlier policy directions, particularly related to tighter targeting of social housing. Current discourses about social mix are located within a policy framework for addressing social exclusion, rather than poverty, as was the case in the past, and the efforts to address the multiplicity of issues it encompasses through estate renewal. Within this frame, the concentration effects of social housing are regarded as major problems on estates. Breaking up and deconcentrating social housing to recreate communities with a more heterogeneous socioeconomic mix of residents are seen as instruments to facilitate less stigmatised and more dynamic and cohesive communities. It is envisaged that introducing homeowners to estates will assist in shaping better functioning communities and improve tenants' lives.

In summary, the commonality of the circumstances for appeals to social mix intensifying at particular times is identifiable as a response to fears about the degree of social segregation between the classes. Over time, spatial segregation between the classes has increased or decreased as a result of broader social, economic and political change. Another theme that the historical exploration demonstrated is that the manner in which the arguments about social mix are framed at specific times reflects the dominant interest groups turning to social mix policies as the solutions and the purposes for which they are used.

The dominant interest group debates about social mix

In Victorian Britain, the principal interest groups pursuing ideas about social mix were intellectuals and reformers. Ideals about social mix were linked to allaying fears that the slums in industrial towns and cities, which were associated with concentrations of the working classes, would lead to class conflict and social disharmony. Social mix was conceived as a solution because it provided a rationale for diluting the concentrations of the working classes, rupturing their social solidarity and, in turn, deflecting their perceived potentially threatening behaviours. A related debate was espoused by industrial reformers, such as George Cadbury, about maintaining the health and vitality of the working class as a labour force for the expansion of industrial capitalism. This debate was linked to emerging public health reforms and recognition that the upper and middle classes managed to avoid some of the diseases and epidemics that afflicted the poor. The principal arguments at this time focussed on the grime, diseases and contamination that were associated with concentrations of the working classes in industrial towns and cities. The resolutions were couched in terms of educating the working classes about proper behaviour. This was perceived as achievable through spatial propinquity of the working classes with the middle classes. It was envisaged that a balanced social mix, composed of different classes, would enable role modelling propagated by the middle classes that would improve the levels of cleanliness, morality and health of the poor. In practice, this encompassed a variety of models ranging from upper class volunteer home visitors, to industrial villages where the working classes resided next to the middle classes. The 19th century social activists largely employed the concept of social mix in individualistic and paternalistic ways in their efforts to create a more harmonious and orderly society. The causes of poverty were depicted as individualistic and behavioural rather than systemic and societal. Social mix proffered a convenient device that targeted individual behaviour as the cause of problems of social and urban decline and at the same time left the existing hierarchical and inequitable social system intact.

The main advocates of social mix policies in Britain after the Second World War were governments and urban planners. This was a time of great optimism about economic growth, with the development of the welfare state and social democratic discourse that envisaged universal service provision and redistribution of wealth from richer to poorer citizens through the taxation system. It was argued, for instance, that enabling broad access to public housing would achieve social balance within neighbourhoods, as opposed to the homogeneity of class that would result from targeting it only to the most disadvantaged and high needs groups. Ideas about social mix were put into practice in the UK in the building of new towns. Nevertheless, undertones of some of the earlier discourses from Victorian Britain were also detectable. These were expressed in similar arguments about social mix as a tool to support propinquity between rich and poor or the different classes, and as a means for providing middle class role models to educate the poor about the proper ways to live in society. Nevertheless, in the social democratic framework, these arguments appeared more benign as poverty and disadvantage were seen as a symptom of the deleterious and unequal effects of capitalism.

Internationally, the intellectual debates of the time were more cautious and raised issues about the desirability of creating mixed-class communities. Influential academics in Britain and the US began to reflect on the relevance of social mix policies. Questions were raised about the appropriateness of creating heterogeneous communities, together with questions about the robustness of the underlying ideas used to support the implementation of socially mixed communities. While it was recognised that heterogeneity is desirable where local taxation is the main basis for funding local community services (as it is in the US), it was cautioned that changing social mix could not substitute government expenditure on education, community development programs and welfare support. A dominant argument was that, if the underlying economic and social inequalities attached to class were addressed, then the increased opportunities might naturally lead to greater heterogeneity within neighbourhoods.

> *Arguments about heterogeneity may also distract attention from the need to reduce social distances in income, housing and standards of living between the classes in society as a whole. If such social distances are reduced then the concept of mixed community becomes a more practical possibility. (Heraud 1968: 34)*

Forced heterogeneity, or varying social mix of the different classes within particular neighbourhoods, was identified in some instances as threatening residents' security and causing conflict or disputes between neighbours. Alternatively, homogeneity, rather than heterogeneity, of background interests, values and class was considered essential if contact between residents of neighbourhoods was to develop beyond superficial exchanges to something as substantial as friendship. From the perspectives of this group of intellectuals, the expectations of planners of social interaction and role modelling developing between middle class and poorer neighbours through spatial propinquity were perceived as simplistic and, in effect, advocating physical determinism.

In 1970s Australia, and South Australia in particular, like post-war Britain, the conceptualisation of social mix was inextricably linked by planners and policymakers with broader redistributive ideals and social democratic visions of governments. These ideals aimed to achieve equality of opportunity and social justice through planning and housing policy and major government programs to redistribute services to the less fortunate members of society. Although the theme of role modelling was again evoked, propinquity of the classes was envisaged as a valuable two-way exchange with the different classes to benefit alike. Wherever possible, public housing was envisaged as a stepping-stone leading to home ownership, while situated within a framework of equity and social justice provision. At this stage, the defining characteristic that separated the discourses from the earlier Victorian ideas about social mix, class and role modelling, was the steeping in social democratic discourse. In a practical sense, this amounted to the implementation of redistributive government services and providing funding at the local neighbourhood level to advance equitable access to a range of quality services within particular disadvantaged neighbourhoods. This was perhaps best illustrated by the funding of The Parks Community Centre by the South Australian Government that brought together a variety of critical services to cater for the needs of a disadvantaged community.

In 21st century Australia, the vocal groups advocating support for social mix are once again policymakers and planners. The concerns raised are about using social mix policies as a way of dealing with the administration and residualisation problems on social housing estates, including problems of stigma and antisocial behaviour. These debates about social mix are situated within a conceptual framework of social inclusion that visualises resident integration across different housing tenures at the neighbourhood level as an 'antidote' to social exclusion. The underlying premise is that living with other disadvantaged individuals renders one more disadvantaged, the so-called 'neighbourhood effects', as if poverty is somehow a disease that is passed on from one resident to the next. These effects are often explained in terms of residents' limited access to the opportunities available in broader society, including job networks and role models of appropriate societal behaviour and norms. In this context, the policy emphasis is less on planning for social mix through urban planning and building new towns as it was in the post-war period, and more about reconfiguration and diversification of social mix on existing estates with high concentrations of social housing.

The contemporary expectations for a balanced social mix emphasise the consistent historical theme about the benefits of middle class propinquity providing role models for disadvantaged groups. In the present day, these groups are symbolised by homeowners and social housing tenants respectively. These ideals reflect similar hopes for social mix as those expressed by Victorian reformers and policymakers in 1970s Australia. In spite of the consistency of this theme linking spatial propinquity to role modelling between the different classes, an important reflection is that social mix policies in this contemporary utilisation are removed from earlier government frameworks of comprehensive provision of social housing, community planning and building, and goals of social equity and social justice. The social democratic redistributive ideals advocating collective solutions to poverty, including government programs to redistribute services and resources to the less fortunate in society, which were dominant in the earlier discussions of the Australian policies implemented in the 1970s, are no longer apparent.

While the historical analysis demonstrated that there have been some consistent arguments expressed for social mix, it also showed a constant oversight in the debates, in that the voices of the working classes and the disadvantaged have largely been missing from accounts of social mix policies.

Residents' perspectives about social mix

At the end of the day, accounts about social mix have predominantly been written by social reformers, the educated classes, planners and government policymakers. The voices of the working classes and the disadvantaged that the policies have aimed to assist are largely missing from the debates. A common assumption has been that the former groups know what is best for the latter in managing their lives. The present research investigated some alternative insights about social mix through engaging with the points of view of residents of three regenerated socially mixed neighbourhoods. The premises explored concerned the anticipated benefits of social mix related to reductions in neighbourhood stigma and improved social cohesion between residents from different housing tenure groups. Residents framed their day-to-day experiences of social mix differently from those imagined by planners and housing policymakers and identified a number of other pertinent issues. Some of the residents, most often homeowners, espoused a segregation type of discourse about social mix, in which pockets of social housing were associated with unacceptable social values, stigma and antisocial behaviours. Another frame of reference that was expressed by residents in different housing tenure groups involved an integration discourse. This discourse was optimistic about the different housing tenures in the neighbourhoods and observed the revised social mix as contributing positively to reducing stigma and the poor reputations that were previously associated with the neighbourhoods when they were composed of concentrated social housing.

The interviews with residents also highlighted some of the outdated ideals on which the policies are based, and the lack of relevance that social mix has to much of their daily lives. Residents' lifestyles are no longer bound to the geographical spaces of their local neighbourhoods like they were in bygone eras. The internet, social networking technology, more flexible workplaces, the entry of women into the workforce in large numbers and the necessity of two incomes to pay home loan mortgages are some of the pertinent factors. These societal changes question the relevance today of the persistent ideal over time about spatial propinquity facilitating role modelling through social contact between the different classes. Home ownership is unlikely to be a reality for groups currently entering social housing, as their home owning neighbours frequently identified that many social housing tenants experience complex social and behavioural issues. From the perspective of many homeowners, social housing tenants were often tarred with the same brush. This is not surprising given that individuals entering social housing are increasingly high need and complex tenants. Nevertheless, social housing tenants resented this depiction of them as one homogeneous group and pointed out that there is a mix of old and new (or good and bad) social housing tenants that challenges such portrayals.

An interesting finding was that, from the viewpoint of many residents, the private rental tenure was increasingly associated with stigma in regenerated neighbourhoods. The objections raised were about the houses not being well maintained as they functioned merely to obtain rental income for absentee landlords. This finding offers a different perspective to those of government policymakers that support the balance of housing assistance in Australia moving further to favour the provision of subsidies for private rental assistance, and affordable rental housing funded through private landlords, as opposed to social housing supplied through government.

The issues that social housing tenants raised about stigma consciousness were the most poignant. The nuanced accounts of day-to-day life suggested that social housing tenants experienced internalised stigma attached to the tenure, most often in their own neighbourhoods by their homeowner neighbours. They felt unfairly judged by other neighbourhood residents due to their association with the social housing tenure and resented being perceived as different. While social housing tenants often expressed support for social mix, the impact of housing design was acknowledged as the principal factor that helped them fit into the neighbourhood. Access to new or upgraded housing that was less identifiable as social housing appeared to some extent to ameliorate this primary level of stigma consciousness from occurring. Merely concealing the discreditable status of social housing from the eyes of their neighbours acted as an impediment to stigma being attached to individuals. The nub of the issue was that the social housing tenants were no longer easily identifiable.

Like policymakers, residents of the three mixed-tenure case study neighbourhoods perceived tenure mix as a proxy for socioeconomic mix. They talked interchangeably about social housing, poverty and disadvantage and utilised the variety of terms as if they were analogous. In other aspects, though, residents' conceptualisations of social mix were different to those adopted by policymakers. Overall, residents tended to depict social mix in more complex ways than policymakers. They illustrated that, on the whole, there is a level of complexity that is glossed over in policy debates about social mix. In particular, residents showed no awareness of policy discourses that linked social mix to social inclusion and exclusion. However, they did highlight that, for them, social mix represented the range of ages of residents in the neighbourhood, along with the mix of children and new and old social housing tenants.

The views of residents, at least in the three case study neighbourhoods investigated, bring a different perspective to policy debates by challenging the contemporary consensus in housing and urban planning that social mix is an optimum planning tool – particularly the underlying rationales drawn on to support contemporary social mix policies. These include the expectations related first to role modelling and middle class leadership to integrate problematic residents into more 'acceptable' social behaviours, and second the linking of resident heterogeneity with increased social cohesion and social integration.

The unintended consequences of social mix policies

Another aspect that is largely glossed over in current debates is consideration of some of the more perverse consequences of social mix policies that raise questions about the end results for disadvantaged residents. As highlighted by the historical exploration, academics in the 1950s raised a number of important issues, many of which are still applicable today, although they receive less interest internationally now than they did then. Young and Willmott (1957: 166), for instance, cautioned against focusing too much on making changes to bricks and mortar to the detriment of respect for the bonds and ties of existing communities. These issues about established communities with long-term social connections between residents that are disrupted through the dislocation of tenants have received little attention in contemporary policy debates. Yet there are key tensions in the housing authorities' social mix policies between the aims to develop more cohesive and sustainable communities and at the same time breaking up and spatially reordering existing communities. Other perverse consequences of contemporary social mix policies include reductions in overall numbers of social housing stock and the loss of benefits provided in terms of affordability and security of tenure compared with private rental housing. Questions were also raised about whether policymakers are merely moving problematic tenants from one neighbourhood to the next and thus relocating rather than addressing antisocial behaviour and other issues.

Do social mix policies tackle causes or effects?

All of this leaves us with the unresolved question of what social mix policies really achieve. The most conscionable argument against the policies is that an emphasis on concentration as the problem in disadvantaged social housing neighbourhoods and social mix as the solution mixes up cause and effect. Arguably, concentration of social housing or lack of social mix is not the casual agent of the stigma attached to social housing, poor reputations of neighbourhoods or a lack of social cohesion experienced within some communities. The concentrations of disadvantaged tenants, stigma and other problems are visible reminders of the consequences or effects of income and other inequalities. Focusing on lack of social mix at the local spatial level is at the expense of neglecting the macro-sociological perspective. The causes of the problems, as has been highlighted, are the impacts of economic restructuring and associated job losses, particularly in manufacturing industry, along with increasingly tighter targeting of social housing, with many residents now subsisting on government assistance. An increasing emphasis on implementing social mix policies to the distraction of addressing inequalities in income and access to services can never be an adequate solution for the complexity of these issues. There needs to be greater emphasis on accepting the 'inconvenient truth' instead of the 'comfortable spin' about the evidence for social mix policies (Bond *et al.* 2010). A more productive application of energy requires exploration of the underlying processes that lead to inequality, so that the causes rather than the effects can be addressed. The incongruity of the arguments is highlighted by considering the link between social mix and stigma.

In contemporary debates there appears a degree of acceptance across governments that social mix policies are a magic bullet and that they will help to fix the stigmatisation of social housing. Certainly it is a worthy aim to address this issue, as in the interviews social housing tenants expressed the seriousness of the effects that the stigma attached to the social housing tenure, and by association with them, had on their lives. Nevertheless, residents illustrated that the mechanisms surrounding the development of stigma and the relationship to social mix are more complex than the policy debates indicate. It seems that in mixed-tenure neighbourhoods the stigma attached to social housing remains but it is processed at a different scale. The discourses suggested that the identification with stigma moves from the whole neighbourhood to a narrower focus, in which individual social housing tenants that were readily identifiable were demarcated and labelled by their home owning neighbours. To some extent, better housing that blends into the community and is not identifiable as social housing prevents the stigma occurring or masks it for individual tenants. However, in reality, the stigma attached to social housing is unchallenged and remains intact. In this respect, the findings also highlighted how notions of normalcy and deviance operate. As social housing has become associated with only the least powerful population groups and increasing levels of inequality, it has become constructed as the deviant housing tenure. In turn, this has amplified the social distance between social housing and the home ownership tenure, which is depicted as normal and desirable. This distinction is especially marked in Australia where home ownership has long been the preferred tenure and is part of the national psyche. As long as these vast divisions remain, any expectations about role modelling occurring between residents across different housing tenures appear ever more utopian.

The targeting of social housing is a key determinant of these divisions and epitomises an important policy conundrum; contemporary social housing access and targeting policies are incongruous with policies to devise a more balanced social mix within areas of concentrated social housing through spatial reordering of tenants. The progressively tighter targeting of access to social housing has also created the conditions in which the stigmatisation of social housing has thrived. The steady reversal over time in the eligibility criteria to house only those in greatest need means that low-income, working families that were originally housed in the past are almost assured they will not get housed in social housing today. This is because their need is not perceived as urgent relative to other groups, including those with substance abuse problems, homelessness, mental health issues and ex-prisoners. However, this situation ensures that there is not a social mix within the social housing tenure, at least in terms of the socioeconomic characteristics of tenants.

The key debate common in the post-war years, missing in contemporary debates, is that social mix can develop more organically through the provision of universal access to social housing and other public goods provided by governments, including health and education. Collective access to public goods is an important source of social inclusion because it provides: a sense of shared values through engaging the more advantaged with the less privileged; broader electoral support for the services; decreased stigma in utilising them; and financial viability of services, as better off users subsidise those less prosperous (Walzer 2007). Residualisation of the social housing tenure and accompanying lack of investment over the years has ravaged any sense of solidarity because as individuals grow further apart they lack a sense of shared fate (Self 2000). As long as the current narrow targeting of social housing continues, approaches to social mix that place homeowners in propinquity with social housing tenants will likely fail. There appears a clear connection between residualisation of the social housing sector and the level of stigmatisation. This is obvious in relation to changes in the base of social housing in Australia over the past 40 years or so but also in the fact that stigma is less a feature of the social housing of Scandinavian countries where there is a broader based and more equal societal context.

Overall, the historical exploration of social mix policies undertaken here illustrated that whether social mix policies are harmless or harmful depends in part on the social and political context in which they are situated. There is a danger that, in the contemporary context of residualisation of social housing and the emerging problems of antisocial behaviour on some housing estates, the call for implementing social mix policies in Australia will draw on earlier Victorian discourses about fear of the poor and their aberrant behaviour. The risk is that policies will be developed that emphasise the need to manage the behaviour of disadvantaged housing tenants through dispersing concentrations of residents at the risk of ignoring wider societal factors that cause inequality. If we are serious about addressing the problems of concentrated poverty and social exclusion then a middle ground must be reached that balances and recognises the critical interaction between broader structural processes and local agency. We must challenge the assumption that poverty is a communicable disease that can be cured by a large dose of social mix.

References

Bond L, Sautkina E and Kearns A (2010) Mixed messages about mixed tenures: do reviews tell the real story? *Housing Studies* **26**(1), 69–94.

Heraud BJ (1968) Social class and the new towns. *Urban Studies* **5**(1), 33–58.

Link B and Phelan J (2001) Conceptualising stigma. *Annual Review of Sociology* **27**, 363–385.

Self P (2000) *Rolling Back the Market.* Macmillan Press, London.

Walzer M (2007) *Thinking Politically, Essays in Political Theory.* Yale University Press, New Havem, CT, USA.

Young M and Willmottt P (1957) *Family and Kinship in East London.* Routledge and Kegan Paul, London.

Index

www.ingramcontent.com/pod-product-compliance
Lightning Source LLC
LaVergne TN
LVHW060623110826

845147LV00015B/924

9780643096424